DON'T DIE
ON THE MOUNTAIN

2ND EDITION

D0557228

By Dan H. Allen

Diapensia Press, New London, New Hampshire

ISBN   0-9662690-0-4

LCCN   97-095034

The picture on the back cover was taken by Tim Allen, and Photograph 6-1 was taken by George Howe. All other photographs were taken by the author. The digitized map and perspective views of Tuckermans Ravine were created by Tim Allen. All other drawings were by the author.

Published in the United States by Diapensia Press, 120 King Hill Rd., New London, NH 03257-4411

This book is dedicated to the next generation of hikers, and particularly to:

Dan, Diana, Cyndi, Justin, Kristoff,
John, Keegan, Jeremy, Konrad, Jay,
Laura and Bennett.

PREFACE

The purpose of this book is to help you enjoy safely the marvelous, above timberline region, and walks in the woods. It is my sincere hope that as many people as possible will benefit from this book and that we will have fewer deaths in the mountains. While I have aimed most of what I have to say toward the beginner, there is much here that any reader may not find elsewhere.

Twenty-six years have passed since the first printing of the first edition of this book, which was written for the Mountaineering Committee of the New Hampshire Chapter of the Appalachian Mountain Club. In excess of 10,000 copies of the first edition booklet were sold, or distributed to new members of the NH Chapter. Now, it is time to recognize the many changes that have occurred, particularly in the gear available: Gore-Tex ®, synthetic pile, polypropylene, metal-framed snowshoes, and plastic boots. As important has been the introduction of the analysis of decision making styles and group dynamics into mountain leadership training.

Each of us has his or her own way of looking at mountaineering and way of doing it. What follows is one man's view of some aspects of mountain travel, definitely influenced by the suggestions of the many people who have read drafts of this and the first edition. To the following people who have reviewed drafts of this second edition and who have offered hundreds of suggestions incorporated herein, both about content and style, I extend my deep felt appreciation: Neal Anderson, Dugald Arbuckle, Bob Dangel, Natalie Davis, John Dunn, M.D., Dave Harrigan, George Howe, John Mudge, Chuck Kukla, Rick LaRue, Lee Manchester, Nancy Rich, Steve Piotrow, Lee Tibbert, Guy and Laura Waterman, Roy Westerberg, and Ruth White. I extend my sincere thanks to my son, Tim, for his help with computer efforts and for creating Figures, and to his wife, Wendy, for her help in book layout. I am very grateful to my wife, Natalie Davis, who did the preliminary editing and to John Dunn, M.D., who did the penultimate editing.

Please address comments and suggestions to me.

Neither the author nor the publisher can be responsible for any calamity that might befall you in the mountains. Even the best advice we can give will not alert you to all the possible hazards there. The principal message in this book is that you alone must take responsibility for your decisions and actions.

Dan H. Allen

TABLE OF CONTENTS

INTRODUCTION

This book was written for beginners and others who want to know what makes the difference between safety and disaster in the mountains. Chapter 1 contains the key to staying alive. It should help you understand how decisions are made and that *your* decisions are so important. Chapter 2 contains a discussion of leadership. Also in this chapter you will find a section that lists the responsibilities of the follower. Chapter 3 deals with the practical aspects of leading a hike, even if you are alone. The remainder of the book provides enumeration of the hazards found in the mountains along with remedies and helpful suggestions. This is information needed by all hikers.

Loafing along above timberline on a warm, clear, sunny day is an incomparable experience. However, the weather changes, people tire, and sometimes they stick too rigidly to their original trip plans. All too late they discover that a hazard is facing them. As either a leader or a follower, you need to be aware of the life threatening situations and how to deal with them by making safe decisions.

Though there are many decisions for the mountain hiker to make, those which you must continuously address, with a view both to the present conditions and those in the foreseeable future, are:

1) Do we have and are we employing the right clothing and equipment?
2) Do we have enough energy and skill?
3) Are we eating and drinking enough to match our rates of energy output and liquid loss?
4) Should we modify our objectives in view of the time, the weather and the pace?

This book addresses what you should know to make the necessary decisions. The choices might depend on many factors.

While most beginners hike in the summer, the extremes of weather above tree line reveal little distinction between seasons in terms of danger. Much about winter hiking can apply to extreme summer conditions. I do not intend to encourage beginners to do winter hiking, but I have said a lot about it because disasters occur in the winter as well as in the summer. Neither the beginner nor the expert will find much technique instruction here. On the other hand, there is much information here you will not find elsewhere, particularly regarding the cognitive aspect of travel away from roads and immediate rescue.

Enjoy the song of the winter wren, the delicate flower of the wood sorrel, and the matchless splendor of a clear day on a high summit. Do it with confidence. Replace your uncertainty with knowledge, skill and experience, and use that as the basis for making good decisions. ❉

1

THE CRUCIAL ASPECT OF SURVIVAL: DECISION-MAKING

A small accident can get you into big trouble when you are wilderness skiing, white water canoeing, sailing, hiking, rock climbing, or wherever you are out of close touch with sources of help. The difference between the real disaster and a satisfactory outcome is the accident. In many accidents the hazard plays a passive role. You cause the accident by choosing to go to the hazard and by being careless or taking large risks.

DECISION-MAKING

To avoid calamity on the mountain you must employ good judgment. Your decisions are the key to coming back safely. After an accident in the mountains the critics carefully examine the poor decisions leading up to the event. You could avoid such accidents by looking critically at your decisions while there is still time to do something about them.

When I talk about decisions and leadership, do not think of the leader as some third person. If you go to the mountains alone, you must make the strategic decisions of a leader, necessary to preserve your life. If you take a friend into the mountains, you will be expected to be the leader. If you go with a leaderless group, then you should make certain that the group addresses the strategic decisions. Making certain that sound decisions are made is the crucial aspect of good mountain leadership.

If you are a beginner, and I talk to you as a leader, you may feel uneasy. Everyone going to the mountains should think like a leader. This and the next chapter are intended to give you some insight into how and what a leader should be thinking. The critical message is that, unless you are in an organized group with an appointed leader, you must take responsibility for leadership. Even in an organized group, you should carefully consider the leader's decisions.

During trips above timberline, decision-making goes on continually as you choose places to put your feet, decide when to eat, assess the potential for a thunderstorm and select which garment to wear. To avoid disaster on the mountain, you must use good judgment. In my concept **good judgment is the making of cautious, responsible decisions involving optimum use of critical thinking.** Critical thinking is the winnowing of information to select the facts, particularly cause and effect relationships, relevant to the issue at hand. Do this objectively, making careful, exact evaluations, discriminations and distinctions. It is not fuzzy, hasty, sloppy, or romantic thinking. By optimum use I mean that the decision-maker gives enough thought so as to look at all the options, but not so much thought (time) that the significant delay would lead to further problems.

Being cautious means evaluating risks, a topic that a later section will address. The meaning of responsibility is addressed at the beginning of Chapter 13.

We can break decision-making down into four steps:
1) Recognizing a problem or question,
2) Recognizing all of the possible solutions (or answers) and their associated risks,
3) Selecting a possible solution, and
4) Initiating the selected course of action.

As an example of decision-making, consider the pause before you take the step across a void. You should ask such questions as: Can I make it weighing a total of 230 pounds (including my pack, boots, parka, etc.) when I only weighed 165 pounds this morning? You cannot do as much when you are heavier. Are the rocks stable where I propose to land? Is the rock surface greasy, because of a damp organic (lichen) coating on the rock? Do I have sufficient bone strength to withstand an awkward landing?[1] How bad are the alternatives? Each of these questions

---

[1]The person who exercises regularly has greater bone density and strength than the person who is basically sedentary.

demands a decision. Whether you should cross the gap depends on your answers. As you answer each question you must carefully evaluate the associated risks. Remember: good judgment is the making of cautious, responsible decisions involving optimum use of critical thinking.

You need to be objective (not subjective) in making good decisions. Consider the question, "Does the appearance of the sky suggest rain?" When viewed critically, you see the present state of the sky in relationship to the recent conditions, the changing temperature, and the wind strength and direction. You rely on your experience by asking: "Have I seen this sequence of conditions before?" Only after looking at all the information available can you make the best objective decision.

Two major categories of decisions are: strategic and pedestrian (I could use other labels). Strategic decisions are those made about the strategy to be employed, such as which trail to take, the turn around time, whether or not to put on crampons, etc. These decisions usually affect all members of the party and the nature of the outing. Often, the leader makes these decisions. As an example of a strategic decision, consider the case of two friends in their early 50's skiing ten miles on logging roads to a cold cabin. The temperature is -5 degrees F., and there is a 15 mph breeze. The sun has set. Three miles from camp, after passing over the hilly terrain, the novice skier is very tired, and is plodding along with no glide. The experienced skier, carrying the one sleeping bag (the other is in camp), contemplates whether or not to go ahead to start a fire, or to remain with the novice. This is a strategic decision, because it is a choice between two very distinct plans of action or strategies.

Pedestrian decisions are decisions about ordinary, repetitive behavior (including walking). Each hiker makes his own pedestrian decisions. Examples are where to place your feet, when to stop, what to put on your head, whether or not to take off a layer of clothing.

The boundary between strategic and pedestrian decisions is not well defined. Certainly, pedestrian decisions can affect your survival. There will be a mix of the two types of decisions in the scenario in which poor decisions lead to serious hypothermia. A hiker immobilized by hypothermia cannot reverse his or her own condition. Strategic decisions will bear on what you try to do in the cold environment, and the minor decisions about when to add and remove clothing will be pedestrian.

When you walk on a trail at higher elevation, the treadway is full of rocks, and you have to give your full attention to the matter of foot placement. As you continually make these pedestrian decisions, you must stay mentally focused. If you lose concentration, you are likely to stumble. This is in contrast to being at home or at work where, in most cases, you can just put one foot in front of the other. You do not have to think about it until you go up stairs or over a curbstone. The pedestrian decisions in mountain hiking often require more thought and alertness than are required in many other forms of recreation.

When you watch a beginner slowly and carefully pick his or her way along a rough trail, you should recognize that the beginner is making those foot placement (pedestrian) decisions more slowly than a seasoned hiker. This is because of the lack of experience (inability to immediately recognize low risk solutions) and a wish to minimize risk. It also happens that some experienced people go more slowly over rough treadways than their fellow hikers. This may be due to slower processing of decisions, eyesight problems, stiff legs or other interferences.

Lone hikers, group leaders and leaderless groups should frequently evaluate whether or not the hiker or the group should continue to go higher on the mountain. This is a decision usually made on the spot based on the conditions at hand:

1) The weather at the present time as well as in the foreseeable future,
2) The clothing and equipment available,
3) The morale and interest of the group,
4) The amount of daylight left,
5) The pace, and
6) The stamina of each group member.

Impetus for that decision comes from changing conditions. The recognition of the need for a decision and the fact that a decision is made is crucial. The leader should also be monitoring closely (asking and observing) how well each group member is taking care of his personal decisions about clothing adjustment, food and water intake, foot placement, blister prevention, etc. The experienced hiker knows that he or she must:

1) Review all the questions related to survival,
2) Evaluate the current situation, and
3) Make decisions about what must be done,

even when preoccupied with a rescue, slippery going or horrendous weather. It is a discipline.

When you undertake activities that involve more risk than that to which you usually expose yourself, you need to be more alert and careful. The safety of the hiking party depends on everyone remaining alert and open-minded. You know what it means to be alert, but think about what it means to stay quite alert all day long. Many accidents happen late in the day when people are tired. Certainly, there is a big difference between being alert, and becoming numbed to the conditions around you by the repetitive foot placement problem. Late in the day we often find ourselves daydreaming, or, at least, making less refined decisions. Sometimes we avoid strategic decisions altogether. This is **cognitive fatigue**. So, it is important to remain alert to your mental condition. You may not be able to do much about tired muscles, but you can do something that contributes to being alert and making better decisions. Eat a candy bar. Keep your blood sugar level up by eating sufficient calories to compensate for those you have burned. Equally important is remaining hydrated, since dehydration results in a reduction in the blood volume, a reduction of the amount of blood available to carry nutrients and oxygen to the brain. Bring plenty to eat and drink. Do not delay eating and drinking. Rather, keep your energy level up throughout the day. Especially late in the day, it is important to not be casual about where you place your feet and how alert you are. Watch what the others in the group are doing. Make the right decisions. Take action. Most importantly, stay mentally focused on what *you* are doing.

In order to recognize the more significant problems one must:
1) Be alert,
2) Recognize problematic or potentially dangerous situations (even those which are not so obvious), and
3) Look for unforeseen problems which result from the selected course of action.

The ability to recognize problematic and potentially dangerous situations depends on the collective intelligence, knowledge, alertness and experience of the people in the hiking group, not just the leader.

It is important to stop and emphasize, again, that *you* should be thinking like a leader.

Remember that decision-making involves several steps, the last of which is taking action to implement the decision. Failure to act results in **impotent decisions**. This is not equivalent to **absent decision-making** (avoiding decision-making), since in the case of impotent decisions the hiker will be aware of conditions requiring a decision and the possible courses of action. Sometimes we put off acting on decisions, waiting for some criterion to be met. These are **delayed action decisions**, which, through neglect, can become impotent decisions. In some cases the correct choice may turn out to be to not act.

Sometimes we vacillate, unable to make up our minds. Usually this results from insufficient confidence that we have identified all the possible choices and their realistic risks. When we are unable to make up our minds, it is often for lack of the particular experience that might have provided us with a better understanding of the choices and their risks.

RISK ASSESSMENT AND MANAGEMENT: Risk is the probability of an undesired consequence of an action. The amount of risk usually depends on the physical hazards involved, but the risk usually decreases as the experience, knowledge, skill, equipment and physical strength of the hiker improve. So, the risks are greater for the inexperienced hiker, particularly when alone. A danger to the beginner is that he or she may not know or understand the risks of an action.

Let us look at what might happen if you have some understanding of the risks but you ignore them.

In January of 1994 Derek Tinkham died near the summit of Mt. Jefferson (New Hampshire) in horrendous weather conditions, with temperatures well below zero and very high winds. Derek was exhausted. His hiking companion continued on to the Mt. Washington Observatory in search of help. The rescuers characterized the weather as the worst they had ever encountered. Published accounts quote the survivor as saying that the pair was seeking the great challenge of horrendous mountain weather. These two college students were driven by a desire to try themselves in the worst possible conditions. From the survivor's statement it appears that they were goal-driven to the point of ignoring risk.

It was reported to me that Tinkham's pack weighed at least one and one half times as much as his companion's, and that they had three liters of liquid with them in their packs that they had not touched (personal communication from Guy Waterman who carried the packs down from the summit of Mt. Jefferson). News reports stated that Tinkham had a down jacket he did not use in the severe weather, because of his fear that it would become soaked with sweat and thermally inefficient.

The hikers could have dealt with the pack weight issue at the trailhead. In 1993 a party starting a winter traverse of the same Presidential Range refused to go until one of its members reduced his pack weight of 76 pounds by removing 10 pounds of non-essentials. It is important to see that too much weight (or too little) can be a hazard.

The implication that these two hikers did not stop to drink water suggests that the conditions were too severe for them to do so. Note that the water bottles were in their packs and not inside their clothing. To travel in conditions that produce dehydration, and not drink, is a severe risk. Dehydration can increase the risk of hypothermia, exhaustion, frostbite, cramps, headaches and loss of the sense of well-being.

While most of you may not be hiking in the winter, you may encounter severe weather conditions above timberline in the summer. The decision-making process is the same. We need to look beyond the Tinkham tragedy at how one would avoid calamity by making appropriate, risk-driven decisions.

Risk assessment refers to the process of evaluating the seriousness of the risk associated with a contemplated action. Risk management refers to the search for alternative actions with lower risk, or means of mitigating the risk. Recall the example mentioned earlier in this chapter about the problem one faces when there is a big step across a gap that, potentially, might have dangers hidden in the landing zone. I mentioned there that good judgment involves the evaluation of the acceptable risks (risk evaluation) in the process of decision-making. In risk management, after considering the possible actions with their associated risks, one chooses those actions with risks that are acceptable. One of these selected actions can be chosen on the basis of how well it matches the agenda.

Factors to consider when making a risk assessment about some contemplated action in the mountains include: the skill required, your skill, your experience with this task, the dangers involved, probability of failure, and the consequences of failure.

In the gap crossing example you may be comparing a slight negative outcome (more work going around the gap) and a high probability of success against a much higher damage outcome (broken bone) and a much higher probability of failure (sliding off the far side). However, the probability of sliding off depends on many factors: the weight you are carrying, the slipperiness of the landing spot, your energy level, your mental state, and your experience making such jumps.

For every physical activity a person undertakes there is some risk of an injury. For most everyday activities the risks are slight, and we take it for granted that we can undertake the activity without appreciable risk. The exception occurs when special circumstances apply, such as an ice coating on the trail. Risk, or the probability that the undesired consequences will occur, can increase as conditions change. As an example, in the summer the fact that a trail becomes wet in a shower might considerably increase the risk of sliding or falling.

Risks to an individual hiker depend on the hiker's strength, skill and stamina. However, the individual's equipment might also affect the risk. For instance, without crampons, considerably more skill is required to negotiate a trail through woods in winter when the treadway is filled with ice, particularly when descending.

In the mountains we are exposed to steep terrain, unstable rocks, slippery surfaces, changeable weather, etc. How can one assess risks, if he or she has no experience with these conditions? Many beginners get into trouble because they assume the special hazards are surmountable at slight risk, and because they have seen other hikers make the passage. Ability to judge the difficulty of the terrain and the risk of falling comes with experience. The skill to deal with the hazard also comes with experience. One should not assume he or she can safely walk where a highly skilled rock or ice climber might prance.

The accomplished hiker finds it tempting to assume the risks are small, because of his or her extensive experience and skill. The experience and skill are never infinite and the risks never vanish. In fact, as you grow older and more experienced, you begin to lose balance and agility. Experience cannot overcome the increased risk due to such loss, and new skills cannot entirely compensate. The risk can be managed to some extent by aids, like ski poles and bifocals.

A person can go someplace he has not been before, and make a sensible risk assessment, if the new terrain has features with risks similar to those of places he or she has encountered before. The cautious approach is to assume that there will be new hazards. For example, climbing on metamorphic rock in the Northeast may prepare you for the mechanics of climbing similar rock in the Southern half of our country. It will not teach you to anticipate poisonous snakes found there on warm ledges.

Risks may occur in unforeseen ways. A late start might result in an after dark finish. Mountain travel on a dark night without a light can be almost impossible. If one finds out only after dark that his or her headlamp does not work, then one encounters an unexpectedly high level of risk. On one trip a hiker broke his ankle partly because the victim's wife's headlamp did not work. He concentrated on shining the light for her and did not pay sufficient attention to the ice on which he stepped. Another example of unanticipated risk occurs with the loss of visibility when an upslope fog (cloud on top of a mountain) forms quickly leading to difficulty in route finding. This can occur when you are already a long distance from distinguishing marks along the route.

In using good judgment, or evaluating risk, it is very important to eliminate consideration of agendas and lists of peaks (goals). One should steel oneself against the seduction by the exotic alpine environment. Make risk-driven decisions.

In Jack London's short story, "To Build A Fire," a man goes out alone in 75 degree below zero weather, against recommendations by his seasoned colleagues, and manages to fall through the ice into a stream. His attempts to build a fire are unsuccessful, because of the difficulty of doing so on snow in cold weather. His dog deserts him. Ultimately, he gets a small fire going. However, snow drops from a tree and puts the fire out, and his fingers become too numb to manage matches. London expressed the opinion that the protagonist lacked imagination, and failed to see the consequences of each unfortunate decision as he succumbed to the cold of the Far North. There are several lessons that are relevant to winter travel, but the most important is to apply foresight to all wilderness travel. We can do this by anticipating what could happen and evaluating the risk.

Hikers often fail to assess how the risk they undertake has a bearing on others. Their loved ones and rescuers may have to accept emotional and physical pain as a result of the risks the hiker takes. Many years ago Albert Dow, an experienced rescuer, died in an avalanche on Mt. Washington (NH) while searching for a pair of lost ice climbers.

Decision-making, with risk assessment, is a mind game. You have to be alert to play. Loss could be total; you could die.

LUCK: You may have been lucky in the past. It is important to recognize two quite different kinds of luck. The first is **dumb luck**. It occurs when you come safely through conditions that might have led to the death or injury of someone else, all other factors being equal. Probably, you did not know the hazards or have the skills to manage them. We call it dumb luck when no intelligence has been used to avoid or manage the risks.

When we assess risk in terms of probability, we realize that there is some chance that we will not be able to avoid the undesirable consequences of the risk. We consider ourselves lucky when we do reach the peak and return safely without coming to grief. This is **calculated luck**.

The object in hiking and climbing is to reduce the risk as much as possible by means of training (skill and knowledge) and equipment. At the apex of mountain climbing, such as practiced on Himalayan expeditions, the climber is pushing the limits by taking risks. These cannot be reduced due to the great uncertainty of the weather, the problematical nature of ice seracs, that cannot be avoided, etc. In fact, we know that approximately one in six climbers attempting Everest will die, based on statistics. That is a calculated risk. If you make it down, it is due to calculated luck.

In looking back at how decisions are constructed, it should occur to you that many decisions in everyday life are made without the deliberate evaluation of possible options and their associated risks. Unfortunately, that is so. Surely, you can recall a case of a teenager who has decided to undertake some stunt and has died in the process. All too often we do something because we seek some thrill, or small gain, without evaluating the risk and the alternatives. It takes discipline to think things through before taking action.

DECISION-MAKING IN A GROUP WITH A LEADER

DECISION-MAKING MODES: Decision-making modes and leadership style are not the same thing. There are several decision-making modes that are often thought of as leadership styles; the latter term generally applies to the personality and interpersonal style of the leader. For instance, a leader could be kindly yet very dogmatic (the family doctor?). At the other end of the spectrum, the leader could be brusque but make no decisions. Decision-making is a major part of leadership, but the latter also includes the ability to inspire, counsel, teach, assist, entertain, comfort, communicate, maintain morale, and more.

Four suggested decision-making modes applicable to hiking group leadership are as follows: 1) authoritarian, 2) laissez-faire, 3) democratic, and 4) consulting.

A leader employing the **authoritarian** decision-making mode makes private decisions, and announces the decisions or issues orders. Autocratic managers typify this mode. You expect this of a steamship captain who must have immediate compliance with his instructions, if his ship is to make a safe passage. Many hikers do not enjoy this type of leadership when it is not needed, but they do appreciate this mode of decision-making when a critical situation is reached and there is no time to waste. An example of a situation requiring an immediate decision and action is the sudden onset of severe weather. The party must immediately stop and seek shelter, continue on, or turn back. Another example is the sudden injury of a member of the party when immediate decisions need to be made about first aid and party safety. Under such conditions other modes of decision-making may be inappropriate, depending on the urgency of the situation. Even experienced hikers need decisive leadership in stressful situations.

In essence, the **laissez-faire** leader lets the group's progress take its natural course, with no intervention. In the laissez-faire decision-making process the leader does nothing that would distinguish him or her from the other members of the party. Decisions, or a consensus, emerge without direction from the leader. For a short trip on a sunny day this may be entirely appropriate. On more ambitious hikes involving experienced people, the group might enjoy this decision-making mode when it is interrupted only by brief interjections of other modes at appropriate times. Note that decision-making might take place by consensus in the absence of leadership. The use here of the term laissez-faire means that there is an appointed leader who is allowing decision-making to occur without his or her intervention. A non-active leader is not necessarily unaware of, or unconcerned about, the circumstances at hand.

As an example of mixed modes of leadership, a group of climbers from Boston attacking a serious climb in the West appointed my friend, Dave, the leader. Another friend told me that Dave was indistinguishable from the other members of the team except at one point. Two of the climbers had lead a particularly difficult face. Once they reached the top, they yelled down that they were going off to set up camp. Dave yelled back, "No you're not, you're going to haul loads up this pitch." This was a decision made in the best interest of the group. All the party members readily accepted his interjection of authoritarian decision-making into an otherwise laissez-faire mode.

A special case of the laissez-faire decision-making mode occurs when no decisions are made in the face of changing conditions and peril. I have labeled this **absent decision making.** The difference is that neither the group nor the leader makes a decision when there is a call for one. For example, suppose a group has been modifying the itinerary during the hiking day without the leader's involvement. Suddenly the group finds itself apparently endangered by a forest fire. If this situation is not addressed, the decision-making mode could be labeled absent.

Democratic decision-making involves decisions determined by a majority vote, or a consensus. If a leader employs this decision-making mode, he or she should mediate the discussion preceding the polling of the members of the group. An example is the vote taken at a fork in the trail when the group decides whether or not to go over the summit or take the loop around the summit cone. The leader mediates the process, and must be ready to accept and support the group decision or consensus. However, the decision may be a long time in the making. Usually there is a vote or poll that determines which course of action the group will follow. Prior to the final decision-making, anyone can lobby or inform the group of the consequences of the various options. After the group has made a decision, the group may not be happy with a person who introduces important, additional considerations, unless that person had no way of knowing of this information earlier. Nonetheless, the person should introduce the information, if it is crucial to the decision.

Democratic and laissez-faire decision-making can be achieved by two distinct means: the majority vote or the consensus. In the majority vote those on the losing side may not want to agree with the decision. There are two ways of reaching a consensus. In one variation a consensus is reached when everyone may not agree, but everyone is willing to accept the decision. Any one objection ruins that kind of consensus. The leader only has to ask if there are any objections. In the second type of consensus an obvious majority determines the outcome in spite of minority objections. A wise group will choose the method of reaching agreement before undertaking the critical decisions, or before the hike.

A leader employing the **consulting** mode of decision-making takes time before any important decision to consult with the group members individually, or collectively, before announcing the decision. Most people like to be consulted, unless their input is disregarded without explanation. The consulting leader who is tactful will provide feedback to the group members during consultation and before announcing the decision.

Decisions made by a group, whether through the democratic or consulting process, tend to be better decisions. This is because more thoughts (hopefully, more critical thinking) are presented, and individual inclinations receive consideration and feedback. Another advantage of the group decision is that the participants are more likely to "buy into" the decision as something they helped create.

Leaders employing democratic, consulting or laissez-faire decision-making modes must be open-minded, if those modes are to work. It is important that all members of the group remain open-minded when faced with important decisions. As an example, using a trail for a bailout (alternate descent route) in winter that descends open slabs, may lead the group to the top of an ice covered face. Unless technical climbing experience and equipment are available, the only safe decision may be for the group to climb back up the trail and to take another descent route. Understanding this option is essential. It should be obvious when you look at all the alternatives. Being unwilling to accept the safer alternative, which might require more work, has led to death. Hikers should always be open to the idea that simply continuing on is not always best.

It is possible for the majority of the group members to be wrong. The person with sound reasoning may have to overcome the majority opinion with persuasion, as in the case of the lone juror who must convince the remainder of the jury. Sometimes, you can do this by asking enough questions to explore the facts thoroughly. As a rule, it is safer to rely on group decisions when there is time for discussion by the group members.

Again, a leader may use different decisions making modes under differing conditions, just as his or her leadership style may vary with the situation.

LEADERLESS GROUPS

The average hiker is often in a leaderless group, a group of hikers who do not have an appointed leader. The concern should be: how will the decisions be made? If *you* go into the mountains with a leaderless group, then you should determine that the appropriate decisions are being made by the group. If an individual makes the decisions, he or she is filling the most important of the leadership roles. The role can shift from one member to another within the group. What is important is the behavior or transformation of that group when the conditions warrant strategic decisions, particularly, when conditions become dangerous. Ideally, the individual with broad outdoor experience, and the ability to successfully resolve critical situations, will undertake leadership or, at least, mediate group decision-making. It is maturity (the ability to handle difficult decisions without losing perspective) rather than specialized experience that is usually more important for this role. One hopes that the remaining members of the group will also be sufficiently mature to accept the emergent leadership. On the other hand, if it is the person with mountain miles but little common sense who asserts himself or herself first, the remaining members may choose to reject that leadership. Persuasion of everyone to a rational, safe plan of action is recommended. If you are in a leaderless group, and you recognize that the group should make a strategic decision, then you are the person who should insist that the decision be made.

Sometimes a leader finds himself or herself in over his or her head, and unable to make decisions. The group is then leaderless. The nominal leader should delegate the leadership to someone else. One or more group members must begin consensus building or leadership. If this does not occur, absent decision-making could lead to a disaster.

THE LONE HIKER

If you go into the mountains alone, then you must make the decisions of a leader. There are, at least, three modes of decision-making employed by lone hikers: 1) deterministic, 2) quasi-consulting, and 3) absent. When you make a decision and act on it, this might be called **deterministic**, the equivalent of the authoritarian mode. If you ask yourself, "What would Charlie do?," this is what might be called **quasi-consulting**. We have seen that not making decisions in the face of dangerous conditions could be called "absent decision-making."

Lone hiking has a wonderful appeal to the adventurous. It offers the opportunity to try any route and to make the strategic decisions in an unfettered way. When you are alone, you must rely on your ability to stay alert. There is no one along to pick up on your lapses in attention or your dropped mittens. The lone hiker should fear panic, a condition that blocks out rational thought, comprehension of some dangers, and good decision-making.

The decisions to be made by the lone hiker include both the strategic and the pedestrian. However, the lone hiker can easily be entranced by the ambitious route, working near maximum physical output, and suppressing strategic decisions. Staying tuned-in to all the necessary decisions is a discipline.

Lone hiking is serious business. You could experience a slow, painful death just because of some minor injury that results in immobilization. You have no one to check your cheeks for frostbite, to administer an antidote in the case of anaphylactic shock, to help you recognize the early stages of hypothermia, to lead you out if you become snow blind or lose your glasses, to care for you in the event of food poisoning, or to take charge if you become nearly comatose from diarrhea-induced dehydration or heat exhaustion. Lone hiking involves more of a risk for anyone who does not adequately evaluate his or her physical condition or who under-estimates how much conditioning he or she has lost since the last outing. Another common mistake is self-delusion about the adequacy of some old boots (or other gear), the deterioration of the weather, or the length of the trip.

It is important to understand the big difference between a party of two and a party of one. Make good decisions in either case.

The beginner is at particular risk in the mountains because he or she:
1) May not identify the hazards,
2) May not be aware of the risks,
3) May not have the skills to manage the hazards, and
4) May not have developed the necessary decision-making discipline.

There is also a chance that the beginner does not know how to plan or manage an excursion, and is not familiar with first aid, route finding, or navigation. The beginner should avoid going into the mountains alone.

Good judgment was defined as the making of cautious, responsible decisions involving optimum use of critical thinking. Caution is exercised by evaluating risk. Experience enables you in that evaluation.

There are at least five modes of decision-making used by groups. I have designated these as the authoritarian, democratic, consulting, laissez-faire, and absent modes. Lone hikers use at least three modes: the deterministic, quasi-consulting and absent decision-making modes.

Now that you have been introduced to the concept of good decision-making, after your next hike examine how the decisions were made. Whether you were the leader or not, this is an evaluation you should make. Having looked at what happened after the fact, begin to make the same analysis during the hike when the decisions directly affect the outcome.

What you take with you will have a bearing on your survival. The lightest and most important item you can take with you is good decision-making skill.

Making good decisions is the difference between going on when you should not, putting on that extra clothing before you become chilled (instead of bulling your way onward), eating and drinking instead of waiting for some assumed destination, and making adjustments in the itinerary based on the condition of the participants instead of ignoring them. Just as bad decisions can get you into trouble, the result of not making decisions can be death. Don't die on the mountain; make good decisions! ❋

MOUNTAIN LEADERSHIP
AND FOLLOWERSHIP

MOUNTAIN LEADERSHIP

Again, I wish to emphasized that the *beginner* who goes to a mountain alone, with a friend, or with a leaderless group, will be expected to make the decisions that a leader must make. In a group with a leader everyone should think like a leader. There are three reasons to do this:

1) Your survival depends on it (a series of bad decisions
   could lead to disaster),
2) You want to evaluate the leadership of the person who is
   leading so that your confidence in him or her will
   become well founded, and
3) You should be comparing your thoughts with the leader's
   decisions, and learn by example.

THE PERSONAL QUALITIES OF A MOUNTAIN LEADER:
Generally, when we think of leaders we ascribe characteristics or qualities. Probably, we can all recall leaders with qualities we admire, as well as leaders with qualities that definitely do not make them attractive. Desirable qualities of a leader include: intelligence, knowledge, appropriate physical skills, alertness, critical thinking ability, listening ability, communication skill, self-effacement, self-sacrifice, willingness to make decisions,

humor, team building skills, willingness to give credit where it is due, equanimity in accepting input, organization, emotional control, body language skill, physical attractiveness, concise writing style, and effective speaking style. Many of these qualities make up the leader's personality. The **essential quality** that sets a leader apart is his or her objective and the energy and determination needed to continue working towards that objective while convincing others that it might be theirs as well. Usually, the more attractive the personality and personal qualities of the leader, the greater will be the number of enlistees in the group working toward the same goal. Whether or not it is reached often depends on the energy and determination of the leader.

While we assume the leader's objective is to climb a peak, keep in mind that the leader's major goal is to bring everyone back safe and, secondarily, as content as possible. The leader should focus his or her actions and decision-making on this goal. Decisions made by the leader before the trip and during form the basis for survival and safe return. The classic example of a leader who brought all his men back safe from a failed Antarctic expedition was Ernest Shackelton whose ship sank while trapped in ice. I urge you to read the enthralling firsthand account entitled *Shackelton's Boat Journey*, by Frank Worsley, captain of Shackleton's ship, *Endurance*. If you are unable to find a library with a copy, then look for the book entitled *Endurance* by Alfred Lansing.

There is a middle ground between leaders with all good attributes and those who are unattractive. A mountain leader can have some of the qualities we like, but not all. If your future depends on the leader to whom you are attaching yourself, you want the leader to know, at least, what he or she is doing and how to do it. Leaders do not have to be attractive for you to have faith that they can get the job done. General Patton, of World War II fame, was known as a tyrant. He did manage effective military campaigns.

We think of great leaders as having charisma and leading by strength of personality. Do not let charisma blind you to the need for other leadership qualities. There are leaders we would choose to follow who are unimposing. Yet, these leaders have the skill, energy, determination, and good judgment we expect from the person with charisma.

The leader must not deny his or her own illness or any other **short-coming** that puts his or her followers at risk. The leader should admit shortcomings before the hike and corrections should be accomplished, if possible. For instance, suppose the leaders find after a whiteout envelops them on the summit that neither of them knows what to do with a map and a compass. Clearly, this is bad news to the followers, unless one of them is prepared to do the navigation. Do not get to that situation. Be honest with yourself about your health, skill, knowledge, and physical ability.

CONFIDENCE: Leaders must have confidence. If they do not, the followers will readily sense this, and the followers will soon begin to express their lack of confidence in the leader. As a result, the leader's confidence will be further diminished. A leader can display his or her confidence by making competent decisions, by avoidance of indecision, and by drawing on significant experience to deal with the many minor problems, issues and dilemmas that occur in the course of the hike. A leader gains confidence by resolving difficult situations and by mastering mountain skills. Maturity helps, but it is not necessarily measured in terms of age. Good judgment is essential. The leader relies on a broad base of experience and learning to communicate confidence to her or his group.

PREPARATION FOR TRIP LEADERSHIP: While it is easy to suggest what a leader ought to do and be, it is difficult to determine leadership competence in individuals who have never been in critical situations. The hiker must evaluate his or her own maturity and competence before volunteering to lead. Clearly, knowledge, careful preparation, good judgment, adequate stamina, and a "cool head" are prerequisites. Also, the leader should be in sufficiently good physical condition to have the reserve energy for an emergency.

What a new leader needs most is experience leading. He or she can best obtain this by co-leading with a more experienced leader. Opportunities to do these are available within organized hiking clubs such as the Sierra Club, The Mountaineers, and the Appalachian Mountain Club. While leadership experience from outside the mountains does not provide one with mountain experience and skills, it can teach you how to lead people effectively.

It is important to understand that you should seek as much broad preparation as possible. The following are my suggestions as to the basic practical background for trip leadership.

1) First Aid training or, preferably, Wilderness First Aid training (Red Cross first aid courses are based on the assumption that an ambulance will come for the victim.),

2) Experience as a follower or co-leader at a technical level comparable to that at which you would hope to lead,

3) Knowledge of, or preferably, experience coping with the most severe weather conditions you might encounter while leading,

4) Acquisition of skills in navigation, weather forecasting, and camping under mountain conditions, and

5) Leadership training courses such as those offered by the Appalachian Mountain Club, The Mountaineers, The National Outdoor Leadership School, and The Sierra Club.

If you lead groups for pay, in some states you must have a guide's license.

If you would like to know more about the emotional aspect of interpersonal relationships, a basic component of leadership, and what it is that draws others to leaders, then I recommend that you read *Emotional Intelligence* by Daniel Goleman. The author claims that emotional intelligence is not the same as IQ, but does enable us in our social interactions.

In Chapter 1, I mentioned that the risk of accident to a mountain hiker is reduced as the hiker's skill and experience increase. This same skill and experience also are important to the person evaluating his or her potential to be a leader. How do you know when you have sufficient skill and experience? Here are a few possible criteria (they may not all apply to your leadership situation):

• Can you carry your share of the load (or pack your share of deep snow) going uphill all day, and still have sufficient energy to deal with an emergency?

• Can you deal with medical emergencies, such as heat exhaustion, an epileptic seizure, a compound fracture, a heart attack, serious frostbite, snake bite, etc.?

• Can you make a fire in the rain when morale and, possibly, survival might depend on it?

• Can you deal patiently all day with people who obviously did not come to the mountain trip prepared?

• Can you lead a party down a mountain at night in stormy conditions?

• Can you bushwhack (and navigate) confidently through thick woods?

Notice that this list is not exhaustive and is a partial amplification of the previous list. Also note that none of these criteria depend on technical climbing ability. A group leader is not necessarily the group's technical leader, but he or she does need mountain travel experience and skill.

If the items above are intimidating, please see them as a suggestion that you seek significant experience with other leaders. In some situations you may be able to assemble the necessary skills by enlisting a co-leader whose skills complement yours. However, consider what might happen if you have to split the group.

A mountain leader has a moral obligation to be prepared to handle normal emergencies that might occur.

FOLLOWERSHIP

On organized hiking and mountaineering trips you are either a follower or a leader. As a follower you should know what is expected of the leader in order to understand his or her role. It also helps to know what the various decision-making modes are so that you can understand what is going on within your party. Surviving an outing in the mountains may hinge on the leader's decisions, but decisions made by a follower, or the group, can be just as critical. Usually, the follower's decisions relate to whether or not to speak up about difficulties being encountered or to give other input.

What will make you a good follower? The **responsibilities** include:
1) Making a reasonable decision before the hike as to whether your physical condition, interest, skills and ability match those requisite for the outing,
2) Discussing with the leader before the trip any gear inadequacies, personal agendas, health problems, or relevant limitations,
3) Coming to the hike as prepared as you can be in terms of food, rest, clothing, equipment and physical condition,
4) Arriving at the meeting place on time,
5) Communicating to the leader during the outing, whatever information the leader needs to make informed decisions, including any problems you are having, and

6) Making an effort to be a member of the group by adjusting your pace to stay with the other members, to the
   extent you can, and by participating in group conversation.

Don't be a sheep. Do participate constructively. Add to the collective
alertness.

Any person wishing to join a proposed mountain hike owes it to the
leader and other party members to make the leader aware of any physical
limitations that person suffers. Allergies, heart problems or other serious
medical problems, dependence on medications, physical handicaps, bad
knees, weak backs, etc., are all conditions that the prospective hiker must
disclose for safety reasons. The leader (or the group) needs this information to make decisions. I have heard of a case in which the leader discovered at the trailhead that one of the participants was blind. Had the
leader known this in advance, the leader could have explored with the
blind person the limits of his or her capabilities. It turned out that the
blind person managed well.

No matter what you believe the leader's role is, leaders and followers
can differ in their expectations about leadership. Only when they communicate is it possible for there to be modification of expectations or,
possibly, negotiation.

When a person asks a leader if he or she may join an outing, and
when that person is accepted by the leader, there is an **implicit contract**
between the two that the leader will do a competent job of looking out
for the welfare of the follower, and that the follower will accept the
leadership. Often, neither knows the other beforehand. However, the
agreement is there in spite of conflicts that might develop around personality, agenda or experience. There is also a secondary contract with the
other party members. When you join a hike you implicitly become part
of a self-rescue team that is ready to help any member, and the strength of
that team is dependent on its size.

The follower can break the contracts by leaving the party after announcing his or her intentions to the entire party, and after absolving the
leader of responsibility. In conventional practice, this action is not
considered acceptable, because of the safety concerns. To leave the party
is a big decision with consequences for all party members. Such an action
should be reserved for only those occasions in which life-threatening
conditions are perceived to exist and only after persuasion has been
exhausted. An example might be where a leader insists on continuing up

a ridge as a lightning storm approaches, and you insist on going down a side trail. Remember, that you may be endangering others by leaving. You are part of an interdependent group.

INTERDEPENDENCE

A group of hikers can be completely interdependent or they can be completely independent. There is a continuum of interdependence. The usual expectation is that the group will stay together and help each other at stream crossings, etc., being as interdependent as possible. This is done in order to maximize the potential for a successful outing and the chance of survival of each member. A leader should make the interdependence expectation known at the beginning of the hike.

An example of the totally independent movement of group members occurred on the summit day on Mt. Everest in 1991 when Rick Wilcox and his team members climbed independently. Rick argued that to belay each other they ran the risk of one person pulling another to his death, since the belaying opportunities were poor. The expedition members reached this understanding long before the party reached the Himalayas. So, just as in the interdependent case, a choice was made to maximize the potential for a successful outing. The difference is in the capabilities of the group members. In this example, each member had to have the requisite skills to travel alone, and he had to undertake independent risk assessment and decision-making.

The reader may have seen loosely run church group outings, college outing club trips, summer camp trips, or outdoor experience programs in which the group becomes spread all over the mountain. Sometimes this occurs because:

1) The individual participant is, by design, being confronted with a challenge,[1]
2) Misunderstanding of the capabilities of each individual has lead to over expectations,

---

[1] Placing hikers on their own to build their confidence is a practice loosely adapted from the Outward Bound "solo." The practice is controversial, because often it is not implemented in a way that insures the safety of the participants. In my Outward Bound solo experience, I was provided preliminary training, confined to a limited space, and periodically monitored.

3) The leader just cannot keep in touch with everyone, or

4) The leader has not learned group control or leadership
for that age group.

In each of these cases there is a potential for a great mismatch between the group goal and the individual's capabilities.

Note that laissez-faire leadership does not improve the survival chances for the group member separated from the rest of the group. Usually, the potential for survival and self-rescue is maximized when the group sticks together, regardless of the experience and capability of the members.

CONFLICT RESOLUTION

A leader has many roles quite distinct from decision-making, and one of them is the resolution of the many agendas, both open and hidden, of the various group members. Particularly, in leaderless groups, and in groups of very experienced people, the individual agendas may result in confrontation and the need for conflict resolution. As is described later in the next chapter, the leaders who invite people on specific trips are in the best position to define the objectives and itineraries. The better the leader describes these in advance of the trip, the easier will be the role of resolving group expectations. If everyone knows in advance that the intent is to climb only peak A with a "turn around time" of 2:00 p.m., then there can be little argument about including peak B, which would require a turn around time of 3:30.

The leader should be aware of the agendas of the participants so as to try to accommodate these as long as it is safe and reasonable to do so. Knowing these agendas helps the leader understand how group members are thinking and evaluating risks. However, it is not always possible to adapt to everyone's desires.

Conflict resolution is usually thought of as the art of compromise with a win-win result in which both parties to the conflict get something they want. When you are the leader of a trip with advertised goals, you should be in a good position to sell those goals and the accompanying itinerary. You could think of leadership as including salesmanship. Before you can begin to sell your plan, it is important to evaluate whether or not the chosen plan is appropriate and leads to your confidence in a positive outcome.

The extent to which you are successful in selling could result in one of six possible situations:

1) The other participants could "buy into" your view, adopting it as their own,

2) They could acquiesce, not changing their views, but politely accepting yours,

3) There could be a truce in which they agree to your terms only to get the day over with,

4) You may find you have no alternative but to significantly modify the goals and itinerary,

5) You could be forced into an unfriendly compromise in order to save some semblance of an outing, or

6) The followers could leave the party, in which case you no longer have anyone to lead.

Because you want a safe outcome for your group members, do not let the group dissolve. Remember, do not just suggest your ideas, sell them thoroughly. While you want to persuade the others to accept your goals and agenda, you also want to meet their needs as much as you can. Again, the leader's goal is to bring the participants back safe, and as content as possible.

A successful salesperson must:

1) Listen to arguments,

2) Present soundly based counter-arguments,

3) Remain calm and friendly,

4) Practice persuasion,

5) Remain flexible and creative while incorporating the needs of others, and

6) Employ tact.

Humor can go a long way to save the day, but others might see humor as sarcasm or as being in poor taste.

As in your non-mountain experience, you have to be able to admit it when others have convincing arguments.

If, as a leader, you really make a mistake, such as overestimating the abilities of the group members, then salesmanship may not make up for it.

Personality conflicts often present a difficulty for the leader. You cannot change another's personality. You may be able to minimize the interaction between the two persons in conflict. You could pull one person aside and ask him or her to help by distancing himself or herself from the other person. If this is inappropriate, then you may be able to mediate or lend perspective. It is sometimes helpful to take everyone's attention off the conflict by drawing the focus to unique aspects of the trail, such as rare plants, or to the view of distant mountains. Another possibility is that of involving everyone in group decision-making. It would not the settle the conflict, but it might direct attention to a constructive activity.

If the conflict is with you, then:
   1) Keep calm,
   2) Minimize the arbitrary decisions and pronouncements,
   3) Maintain a friendly approach, and
   4) Maximize adherence to the announced agenda,
      within reason.

Mountain leadership is the art of taking people (including yourself) to the mountains and bringing them back safe. It involves many skills that must be employed in a great variety of situations. The crucial aspect of good mountain leadership is making sure that sound decisions are made both in the planning stage and while leading the hike. On the trail the leader needs to zealously guard the welfare of his followers.

Leaders have personalities and qualities that make them attractive to us. The essential quality of a leader is his or her goal plus the energy and determination to reach that goal while interesting others in its pursuit.

Followers have very important responsibilities to the leader. The followers and the leader have an implicit contract when they agree to accompany each other.

The safety of all members of a hiking group is maximized when all members stay close enough to communicate with each other and assist each other at dangerous locations (maximizing interdependence). ❇

TRIP ORGANIZATION & MANAGEMENT

TRIP PLANNING AND GUIDING

PLANNING: There are two stages to the leader's role in an organized trip: planning and guiding. In the planning stage, he or she first chooses a destination and route (with descent alternatives for adverse conditions, known as **bailouts**) in keeping with the ability level of the anticipated group members. Then, the leader estimates the time and energy required. How long should a trip be? In the summer, hiking eight mountain miles is a good day's work for the average group, though it might not take eight hours. If the treadway is smooth and the elevation gain is moderate, then twelve miles would be manageable for the average group with a whole day available.

Most trail guidebooks include estimates of the normal hiking time for a trail segment, often referred to as **book time**. It is based on several factors. For average hikes, the rate of travel is assumed to be two miles per hour for summer travel, but an hour is added to the travel time for every thousand feet of elevation gain. This assumes there are no complications like ice, snow, difficult stream crossings, unusual terrain, or difficult treadway. Book time does not allow for more than a couple rather short breaks each hour. In cases where the trail is particularly difficult, extra time may be necessary. In winter a lot depends on whether or not some other party has previously packed the trail. A strong party, with little snow to pack, can travel in summer book time. On the other hand, packing ten inches of new snow uphill may take two hours per mile. Alone, I can average about a mile an hour in average winter conditions with a heavy pack, unless the going is easy. Then I can average about a mile and a half an hour, or somewhat faster with only a day pack. Book time is based on hiking time with a moderate backpack. Adjust the estimated times to reflect your pack weight and physical condition.

A challenging bushwhack in woods with soft snow and blowdowns may mean one quarter mile per hour for several hours—four hours to go one mile! On the other hand, you may be able to zoom downhill on a trail in less than half the time it took you to ascend, depending on how smooth the treadway is.

At this point I think it is important to emphasize the difference between Eastern and Western trails. While there are some steep trails in the West, most are graded for horses, have relatively smooth treadways, use switchbacks, and have a steepness (gradient) which seldom exceeds about 15 degrees. Eastern trails often go right up the fall line, can have very difficult footing, may go right over ledges or up brook beds, and can have gradients as steep as 45 degrees.

On the Appalachian Trail between Boiling Springs, Pennsylvania, and High Point, New Jersey, the treadway is intermittently covered by loose rock like a horizontal talus slope. My pace dropped from 2 mph to 1 mph or less each time I encountered these rocky sections.

In the winter, a real trip length limitation is the short day. At the first of the year the time between sunrise and sunset is about 9 hours (Latitude 43 degrees north, near Concord, NH, Pocatello, ID, or Madison, WI). That is not a very long day. Keep in mind that haste due to approaching darkness occurs when you should be slowing your pace. Accidents often occur when you are tired.

With all this in mind, figure out how long your hike will take, allow a margin of daylight at the end, and establish a starting time and a "turn around time." Set the meeting time a half hour earlier than the starting time, and estimate your travel time to the trailhead over slippery, dark roads.

For our purposes the **turn around time** is that time by which you must start back in order to return to the trailhead by a definite time, such as sundown. For winter hikes up a mountain and back the turn around time is usually around 1:00 or 2:00 p.m. If all the hiking is on relatively level ground, the turn around time will be earlier. Always keep in mind that, winter or summer, there is no adequate substitute for an early start.

While speed goes down as the party size goes up, each situation implies some minimum safe party size determined by the requirements in an emergency. If a person becomes injured, certainly one person should stay with the patient while a safe party of at least two people goes out for help. On this basis, the overall size of the party is not so important as the requirement that there be at least four strong people who can fill these roles (assuming one of them becomes injured). If the group undertakes self-rescue, and one person must be carried, the group may have to be larger than four people! However, environmental concerns suggest a maximum group size of ten or fewer (see Impacting the Environment).

When planning or leading a mountain trip never underestimate the impact on yourself or your followers of a sprained ankle, broken arm or other injury that could occur just from a misstep or fall by someone in your party. The injury could occur to someone in some other party that asks you for aid. If the victim becomes immobilized, a race to save the party from hypothermia, particularly the victim, may be your challenge. The immobilization of one person means that all the party members are no longer keeping warm by hiking. You will not have a choice as to where or when the accident occurs. If, when planning a mountain trip, you think about the possibility of such an accident, you will be more cautious and prepared.

It is appropriate for all leaders of mountain trips to take a protective view toward their followers, since the major goal of the leader should be to bring the hikers back safe. Parents taking children with them, and adults taking elderly parents, usually assume this protective perspective. If you are young enough that you have not thought about your own mortality, you should at least consider that the friends you take to the mountains are mortal. You want to guard their lives and welfare with zeal.

Leaders of organized trips should keep in mind that they offered the trips for the benefit of the followers. Leaders must put their followers first, and let their personal agendas come second.

It is often easier to lead experienced people than it is beginners. With beginners there can be a greater mismatch between the difficulty of the trip and the capability of the weakest group member.

Next in the planning process, the leader recruits a co-leader. The leader can expect the co-leader to take over if something happens to the leader, or to lead one group if you must split the party for some compelling reason. The leader then publicizes equipment requirements, necessary previous experience and physical condition, length and difficulty of the trip, and aspects of general interest: natural history, local lore, or attractive vistas. Then, the leader provides a definite meeting place and time that everyone can understand.

If the leader and co-leader have not been over the trails proposed for the trip, or if the leaders have not been over these trails in the recent past, they should do so in advance of the advertised trip.

GUIDING: The guiding stage begins when the leader has a conversation with a prospective participant. The leader owes it to his group to go over each individual's equipment, physical conditioning and experience before the trip. The leader should also discuss the trip goals, itinerary, and any necessary equipment. Sometimes these frank discussions intimidate would-be participants whom the leader should reassure that the trip is within their abilities.

At the trailhead, the leader:
1) Makes introductions,
2) Reviews goals, pace and destination,
3) Assigns trail-finding and trail-sweeping duties, and
4) Specifies how tightly the group must stay together including the expectation that everyone must wait for the group to assemble at trail junctions, stream crossings, etc.

The **trail-sweeper** is the person who comes last and who makes sure the group leaves no one behind.

If the group is to stay together, it *must* travel at the pace of the slowest person. This is a condition of group membership. It is dangerous for faster members to go way ahead of the group, because it breaks communication and interdependence. There may be need of help at the rear of the procession. The forward group may not include the leader or co-leader and may make unjustified assumptions about a goal that is unrealistic for the slowest member. The faster group may even start down the wrong trail without the other group's knowledge. At trail junctions and locations along the trail involving special hazards (such as stream crossings), members should always wait for the whole group to assemble. It is up to the leader to impress on the group members why the group should stay together.

In some cases it is appropriate for the leader to check at the trailhead the specific equipment of people new to him or her. It is appropriate to ask if each member has remembered to bring the essentials enumerated by the leader in the pre-trip conversation (see the checklist in Chapter 11). The leader may want to lift each pack to determine whether or not any pack is excessively light or heavy. Too much or too little gear could be a hazard to the whole group.

After the trip the leader needs to make sure that:
1) There is a debriefing,
2) Addresses are exchanged where needed,
3) Borrowed equipment is returned, and
4) Everyone's car starts and everyone has a ride.

The leader should not rush the closing to the point that people miss saying good-bye to everyone. A spoiled closing can cast a shadow on the perception of the whole day.

SETTING THE PACE

Since some types of torn muscles are most likely to occur at the outset (cold muscles can tear when loaded suddenly), the leader should start the group at a moderate pace that he or she adjusts early on to reflect how group members are doing. He or she should see that the pace is not greater than the slowest member can maintain, nor faster than all would enjoy, since discouragement can set in early.

On many trips the leader must help someone with a slow pace. The slow hiker usually does much better in front of the group rather than behind it. If the slow person is in back, he or she may be depressed by the feeling of both physical and emotional separation from the rest of the group and by the perception that he or she is holding the group back. In front, the slow person may no longer feel this separation, and may be able to put more energy into hiking and less into fretting. The leader may not always be able to ask the slowest person to go ahead. Instead he or she may have to ask the others, perhaps out of earshot, to hike behind the slowest person.

Sometimes a pace-setter who maintains a slow but steady pace can lead the slow hiker in a way that he or she cannot. The fatigued hiker and the hiker who wants to conserve energy can help maintain the leader's pace by taking short steps, none of which require lifting the knee higher than necessary. Going uphill, a hiker can maintain a gait that involves swinging the legs forward and back with only small vertical steps much longer than one that requires more pronounced knee bending. Avoid taking big vertical steps, whenever possible. Small vertical steps are also helpful going downhill, since there is much less pounding that the knees have to absorb. For the beginner, and older folks, this pounding can make the knees very sore.

The slow moving snowshoer may find that ski poles will help both ascending and descending. Ski poles or a walking stick can be helpful to the slow hiker in the summer. The hiker can use these both to help maintain balance and for some thrust when ascending or descending.

Redistributing the slow hiker's load among the other group members does help the slow hiker go faster.

Hikers abort many hiking trips, especially those with ambitious goals, for lack of time due to a slow pace combined with too many stops. The group should keep in mind a timetable and implied rate of travel set by the leader. Going slowly is usually acceptable, but many stops result in a much decreased average speed. In winter, days are so short that each member should minimize the number and lengths of stops he or she must make by saving errands until others stop, or by thinking of possible errands when others are stopping to do theirs. Putting gear in pockets or stuffing it inside your shirt will eliminate a stop. Being able to adjust clothing while underway is a goal worth seeking. Sometimes the hiker can anticipate, for instance, by putting more clothes on just below timberline where conditions are more suitable. Similarly, the hiker can add clothing before reaching the shadow on the middle of a high-angle snow face (shady places are colder and steep slopes are inconvenient places to put on gear). Stops in winter are short, since one will chill rapidly when physical activity stops.

Regardless of goal attainment, hikers should honor the turn around time; hiking after dark is risky. It could lead to a broken ankle or worse.

THERE IS NO ADEQUATE
SUBSTITUTE FOR AN EARLY START!

BEING OUT-OF-SHAPE: It is helpful to a leader to understand what being out-of-shape means and how it affects the slow hiker. Physical activity depends upon the metabolism of glycogen by the muscles.

The liver and muscles store only a limited amount of glycogen. Physical conditioning involves building:

1) The muscles used in the exercise,
2) The glycogen storage mechanism, and
3) The ability to convert stored fat to energy.

Someone who works out in the gym can build muscles without building the energy storage and conversion capacity for an all day workout. For this reason, the best conditioning for all day physical activity comes from all day physical activity. When you are unable to get this kind of exercise, be careful about your expectations. Preparation for a long hike should involve more than planning and packing! See *Smart Exercise* by Covert Bailey for a helpful discussion of what works in physical conditioning. Remember that an all day hike up a mountain and back means heavy work for more than four hours. The average workout at home does not last more than an hour.

One reason for poor performance by an out-of-shape hiker is overheating. The body just cannot put out as much physical work when it cannot get rid of the waste heat energy. Many people are not aware of how much they are perspiring, or they accept it as a condition of hiking. It is important to help these hikers see how important clothing adjustment is. On the other hand, hiking when cold can lead to torn muscles. Encourage others in your hiking party to keep adjusting what they wear.

Another possible problem facing the untrained athlete is improper breathing. When you work hard in an unusually long workout the abdominal muscles, used in heavy breathing, become fatigued. The abdomen should expand as you inhale and contract as you exhale. When you become fatigued there is an inclination to hold these muscles taut or rigid and breathe by expanding other muscles. A much smaller volume of air is exchanged in this type of breathing, and the individual must go slowly, because of a limited intake of oxygen. Worse, the person trains the muscles in an inappropriate way. When this training occurs over a long period the result can be that the person awakes at night in a panic out of breath. This is because the abdominal muscles are held taut and normal breathing ceases. In order to overcome fatigue of the abdominal muscles, consciously expand and contract your abdomen with each breath as you hike uphill. This is particularly important once you have begun to tire. If you have to help a tired hiker, ask the hiker to place his or her hand on his or her stomach. The hiker should then try deep breathing both with the stomach muscles held taut and with exaggerated stomach expansion.

The difference in air volume should be obvious. Next the hiker should determine whether or not he or she is using these abdominal muscles while hiking. Note that a day pack waist strap that is too high, pants that are too tight, or an abdomen full of gas can each interfere with deep breathing.

People who normally do not push themselves physically are often unwilling to open their mouths when working hard hiking uphill. However, the oxygen intake with each breath is substantially greater when breathing through the mouth.

There is no question that a head or chest cold saps the energy of a hiker. He or she is likely to be disappointed by how little energy there is for hiking. Anyone starting out with the remains of a stomach "bug" will probably find that it will not get any better while out on the trail. Followers with a cold or stomach bug should not ignore these; they should stay home. The leader who knows about a follower's cold or stomach bug should encourage him or her to stay home and tell the person why.

MAINTAINING MORALE

At all times during the hike the leader is responsible for maintaining morale, especially during emergencies. The leader should be sure to alleviate the uncertainty followers have about their own abilities, the weather, the terrain difficulties, etc. The leader should be scrutinizing the followers to determine early on who is beginning to limp, who is overheating, and who has a problem with stamina. Any limp should trigger a dialogue. Each problem a follower has with the hiking should bring forth suggestions from the leader. If a hiker is becoming discouraged from lack of stamina, it helps to emphasize how far the group has actually come, or to suggest ways to help that person maintain his or her pace. The leader should let the participants know what each can do, and help them do it. The leader should also make sure that the followers are all eating and drinking enough to insure they have adequate energy.

The leader should know that in an emergency certain activities can give a tremendous boost in morale. One is remaining calm and maintaining an upbeat dialogue. Others are building a fire and providing a shelter. At the same time, she or he must understand that a fire may not warm all of the clothing of a wet party, and wet hikers may not be able to survive a cold night without dry sleeping bags and dry clothes.

Never underestimate the significance of accomplishing your goal as a means to boosting morale. To reach this end, plan well and start early.

ANTICIPATING BEING LOST

When you leave home by yourself for a day at a time, or longer, probably your family expects you to informally check in or out with them. Even if you told friends or family your mountain itinerary, they could not organize an adequate search effort. Such searches require many well equipped, seasoned people familiar with the country they will search. You should let your friends and family know your route and intended schedule and whom to contact in case you do not return on the day indicated. It is very important to be firm about the distinction between the time you expect to be home and the time by which they should consider you overdue. If you expect to be home Sunday at 6:00 p.m. and you recognize the possibility that you might have to spend another night out, then be sure to specify an **overdue time** very late on Monday or early Tuesday. Searches are undertaken all too often when the hiker is not in trouble, but the caring, not-so-savvy relative calls to report that the hiker did not return at the time *expected.*

RESCUE ORGANIZATIONS: In many states the organization in charge of search and rescue is the state's Department of Fish and Game or the equivalent. If you do not know whom to call, call the State Police. The dispatcher will know the correct office to contact. To reassure your family, obtain the correct telephone number for search and rescue operations ahead of time.

If you sign in at a register at a park headquarters before your trip, be careful to sign out when you return. Failure to do so could trigger a search, although there is rarely an automatic response. Usually authorities do not undertake a search until a concerned family member calls. Some states may expect you to pay the cost of that search.

THINGS TO CONSIDER: If you are alone, injured and overdue, the search for you is not difficult, as long as you are on the intended route that is part of the hike plan you left with friends. If you are off trail, the search can become complicated, leaving you two choices: 1) make your way out of the woods, or 2) make yourself conspicuous in one place using noise, bright colors, smoke or any other means of attracting attention. Do not move from spot to spot, particularly once you have made yourself heard or seen. Do not move at night in difficult terrain. If you remain calm, still have lots of energy, and use logic, you can probably get yourself out only a day late. If you become injured on a bushwhack, it may take rescuers several days to find you. If you become frantic, you stand a good chance of becoming injured.

If you are lost in high, glaciated country, ridges are more likely to be navigable as down routes than glacial carved ravine headwalls. In eroded sedimentary areas, down routes are often few and far between. Where they exist animals will use them, and a discontinuous path may be apparent. Ravine (canyon) walls are often miserably brushy and steep. In bad weather it is dangerous to head for higher ground as the way out of trouble. Normally, conditions become much worse with altitude, and require much more energy to overcome. Leaving the trail above timberline, when fog or dark limits visibility, is asking for trouble.

One could argue that a larger party has the greater potential to conduct a self-rescue, provided that all the members are strong enough to contribute. Note that the potential for an injury goes up with the party size. You should not go into the woods with the conscious or unconscious expectation that someone will come and rescue you, if you get into trouble. You must pay attention to the risks encountered in hiking, particularly the ones you are not exposed to in your everyday life.

Before you get into difficulty, consider the ethic involved in sending for help as compared to self-rescue. See the discussion of **Search & Rescue** in Chapter 13. Also see **What To Do When You Are Lost** at the end of Chapter 7.

Mountain leadership is the art of taking people (including yourself) to the mountains and bringing them back safely. It involves many skills that the leader must employ in a great variety of situations. The crucial aspect of good mountain leadership is making sure that sound decisions are made both in the planning stage and while leading the hike. On the trail the leader must zealously guard the welfare of his or her followers.

Anyone planning a hiking trip needs to consider what the participant(s) can manage, what skills are required, and what must be carried.

Trip leaders are often challenged to help someone who is out-ofshape. Being aware of which muscles tire can help the hiker compensate.

The leader should keep in mind that he or she offered the hike for the benefit of and enjoyment by the followers. ❊

NATURAL HAZARDS AND SOME SUGGESTIONS

When you go to the mountains you enter a realm where there are many natural hazards.

This Chapter describes some aspects of the hazards you may not have considered. Note that you choose to go to the mountains in part because these hazards make the trip adventuresome. Hazards imply some risk.

The greatest number of injuries to hikers occurs to those who trip, slip, slide or fall on loose, uneven and slippery footing.

Know the hazards. Be cautious. You must decide when the risk is acceptable. Understanding the problems presented by natural hazards should help you make more informed, low risk decisions. Leaders are responsible for knowing the hazards in their territory, and for providing approaches to these hazards that minimize risk.

WINDCHILL

One of the most dangerous hazards is windchill. The active hiker can usually keep warm by means of exercise, even when conditions are really bad. Even the active hiker can fall victim to the insidious advance of hypothermia. This is particularly true when his or her clothes are damp from heavy exertion. The injured hiker, who cannot keep going in such conditions, soon becomes severely chilled.

	ACTUAL THERMOMETER READING (°F)																					
	60	55	50	45	40	35	30	25	20	15	10	5	0	-5	-10	-15	-20	-25	-30	-35	-40	-45
	EQUIVALENT OR WINDCHILL TEMPERATURE (°F)																					
CALM	60	55	50	45	40	35	30	25	20	15	10	5	0	-5	-10	-15	-20	-25	-30	-35	-40	-45
5	58	53	48	43	37	33	27	21	16	12	7	1	-6	-11	-15	-20	-26	-31	-36	-42	-47	-54
10	52	46	40	34	28	21	16	9	2	-2	-9	-15	-22	-27	-31	-38	-45	-51	-58	-64	-70	-77
15	48	42	36	28	22	16	11	1	-6	-11	-18	-25	-33	-40	-45	-51	-60	-65	-70	-78	-85	-90
20	45	39	32	25	18	12	3	-4	-9	-17	-24	-32	-40	-46	-52	-60	-68	-76	-81	-88	-96	-103
25	43	37	30	23	16	7	0	-7	-15	-22	-29	-37	-45	-52	-58	-67	-75	-83	-89	-96	-104	-112
30	42	36	28	20	13	5	-2	-11	-18	-26	-33	-41	-49	-56	-63	-70	-78	-87	-94	-101	-109	-117
35	42	35	27	19	11	3	-4	-13	-20	-27	-35	-43	-52	-60	-67	-72	-83	-90	-98	-105	-113	-123
40	41	34	26	18	10	1	-5	-15	-22	-29	-36	-45	-54	-62	-69	-76	-87	-94	-101	-107	-116	-126
45	41	33	25	18	10	1	-6	-17	-24	-31	-38	-46	-54	-63	-70	-78	-87	-94	-101	-108	-118	-128
50	41	33	24	17	9	0	-7	-17	-24	-31	-38	-47	-56	-63	-70	-79	-88	-96	-103	-110	-120	-129

LITTLE DANGER FOR PROPERLY CLOTHED PERSONS	INCREASING DANGER OF FREEZING EXPOSED FLESH GREAT DANGER

Figure 4-1: Windchill Graph

The chart above, adapted from material available from the National Oceanic and Atmospheric Administration, shows the chill factor (CF) and the windchill temperature (WCT) as measures of how cold it is. The **chill factor** is the rate of heat loss from exposed skin.[1] By definition, the **windchill temperature** is the temperature of calm conditions that have the same chill factor as windier conditions with a higher thermometer reading. Different wind and temperature combinations with the same WCT are supposed to chill the body at the same rate.

To read the chart, find the ordinary thermometer temperature at the top of the chart and follow that column down until you reach the row associated with the wind velocity, indicated on the left border. The temperature at the intersection is the "windchill temperature" and indicates the temperature for calm conditions with the same chilling effect. All wind and temperature combinations with the same chill factor will lie

---

[1]The unit of measure for the chill factor is kilocalories per square meter-hour. One kilocalorie, as used here and by physical scientists, is equivalent to one calorie as used by the nutritionist. This is referred to as a large calorie or Calorie. The average adult body has a surface area a little less than two square meters. Keep in mind that only a small portion of a properly clothed body is likely to be exposed to severe conditions.

along a chill factor curve. The WCT is not an all-inclusive measurement. Humidity is not a variable on this chart, though it is important. People feel colder when it is damp. Some difference exists between the very cold and very windy conditions with the same WCT. Cold conditions may be worse than windy conditions with the same WCT, since they may actually take more heat from the body through the large surface area of the lungs. However, windy conditions take their toll too, since it is physically and psychologically fatiguing to hike in high winds. High winds may also increase your chance of being blown over and injured.

Going uphill with the wind is easy, from the standpoint of keeping warm, but coming back down into the wind, when not burning up as much energy, can chill you severely. Your relative wind speed may change by as much as six miles per hour assuming you hike at the rate of 2 mph going up and 4 mph descending. At 50 degrees this could change the CF from 200 to 600; at 10 degrees it could change from 400 to 1100! Hikers aggressively pushing their physical limits while traveling to a mountaintop can overreach the protective capability of the clothing they carry, keeping warm by means of physical exertion. They could then find their clothing insufficient once they stop or start to descend. This is particularly true if the weather is deteriorating. Also, the hikers are unlikely to change out of sweat-soaked shirts at the top of the climb where it is wet, windy and cold. Even in the woods the difference between going uphill and downhill can significantly affect the heat you generate as a byproduct of physical activity.

In the author's experience (climbing on days when the weather was not horrendous), the median winter conditions encountered midday on the summits of the 4000-footers in New Hampshire involve a CF of about 1400, or a WCT of -18 degrees F. Recall that the CF is a hypothetical measure of the rate at which the wind can take heat away from the body. The WCT goes down as the CF goes up (they are inversely related).

Hypothermia and its treatment are discussed in Chapter 5.

FALLS AND SLIPPERY GOING

This hazard includes conditions that cause falling, tripping, ankle rolling, slipping, and uncontrolled slides or drops. In all these cases, the more significant injury is likely to occur as the victim reaches the end of the fall. In the case of tripping, the victim who cannot catch himself or herself might receive a serious head injury. Slow your pace when you are tired, buffeted by gusty wind, or on difficult footing. All three conditions may occur together.

On a moderately smooth treadway you can walk fast enough so that your eyes are looking at where you will step many steps later. When the treadway is very rough you have to keep your eyes on each spot on which you will place your foot as you evaluate the risk. You must go more slowly to do this. Keeping yourself focused on those decisions is serious business, particularly late in the day.

Below timberline be particularly cautious regarding exposed roots that loop above the ground. Another trap can occur when you step on a plant stem that is securely fastened to the ground by roots. If the second foot catches on the plant stem between the first foot and the roots, down you will go. If you can hop so as to get the weight off the first foot, you may be able to catch your balance. To avoid falling, make sure each step is deliberate. If you do fall, try to land on your pack.

Rolling the ankle, whether it occurs on the trail or while crossing a brook full of smooth, rounded rocks, can result in a fall to the side that is difficult to correct and which can result in a broken ankle, broken arm, and/or head injury. Again, try to land on your pack.

Look for low spots between rocks in which to place your feet in order to avoid rolling or slipping. Any low spot, or hollow, in a stable rock might do. The idea is that you want to find a spot out of which the foot is not going to slide. Where there are roots on a worn treadway there are usually hollows between them. Where all the boulders in a stream bed are rounded, look for spots between them, or for boulders sufficiently flat that they will not roll over when you put weight on them while you are in motion. On steep grass slopes look for the hollows between clumps of grass. Be careful to avoid side thrusts; keep your weight over your feet. Treat smooth, wet rocks as if ice had coated them.

There are many situations where there just are not enough "buckets" in which to put your feet. If you are on rock with any significant slope to it, this is where you become a rock climber. In rock climbing, footholds often are hollows, but support much less of the foot.

Uncontrolled slides result from loss of traction on steep slopes. Trails often skirt the top of steep slopes, where the views are excellent, and where the slope becomes steeper and steeper the farther off trail you go.

These are not good places to lose your footing! Avoid under-estimating the danger at the top of a cliff.

On two occasions I have found myself sliding where a continued slide would have been likely to result in significant injury. On one occasion I was shoveling snow off the barn roof. In the other case the thin skim of ice on the ledge I was on started to slide with me. In both cases I was able to stop the slide by turning to face downhill, by getting my weight over my feet and letting my Vibram® soles, and my crampons in the second case, do their work. To pull your feet under you, make your feet go more slowly than the rest of your body. This assumes your weight is uphill from your feet. If you are sliding with your feet uphill, drag your arm on one side so as to swing your feet around and downhill. Then you can pull your feet under you. Even if you cannot stop the slide, you will be in a better position to avoid obstacles when standing upright. Try this recovery without crampons on steep, firm snow where there is a safe run-out.

There are several conditions that can make the going slippery, but not too hazardous, on smooth, horizontal ground: wet leaves, frosty leaves, pine needles, pinecones, and acorns. Anyone who rides a bicycle or motorcycle knows how slippery sand and pebbles can be on a smooth surface. In the mountains the substantial hazard exists when these conditions occur on sloping ground above a cliff or other drop-off. Keep your eyes open.

Where you place your feet determines your chances of sliding or of upsetting the rock. Your climbing partner's life may depend on it. Do not let him or her die on the mountain. Make pedestrian decisions carefully. If you need to slow down to make good decision about good foot placement, then do it. Keep your weight over your feet.

SLIPPERY ROCKS: Any wet rocks could be slippery; treat them with caution. Rocks covered with organic material, most commonly lichens, are particularly "greasy." This coating may be a very thin layer of brown, green, or grayish material. Look for the worn surfaces of the rocks along the treadway, which are less likely to have this coating.

A second hazard occurs when rocks are very smooth. They may be smooth because they are very fine grained rocks, such as some igneous rock found in geological dikes, and sedimentary rocks made from silt or clay. Or the rocks may have been worn smooth in stream beds. Smooth rocks lack the surface undulations, or roughness, which occurs when a coarse-grained rock weathers or breaks. Smooth, water worn rocks in stream beds can have a slippery coating of algae that may not be visually apparent. You are more likely to find this coating in shady brook beds above normal water level. Remember, that cold rocks collect condensation on humid days, making them much more slippery than when dry.

SLIPPERY ROOTS AND LOGS: Roots are unavoidable on most trails through woods. They certainly can be slippery when wet. Try to place your feet in depressions rather than on the roots. Logs without bark can be as slippery as roots when wet. Water bar logs, wooden ladders and bog bridges may all become very slippery. They sometimes acquire a coating of algae when in damp locations, which increases their slipperiness. Logs with loose bark are more treacherous, because they do not look slippery. The bark slips off the log when you put your weight on it. You are likely to find these on bushwhacks.

When you step on a dry, smooth root with a wet boot the root will be wet by the boot, and will be as slippery as if it were wet before you stepped on it.

You may find that it is helpful to have a personal policy of, generally, not stepping on roots and logs whether they are wet or dry. Then, you will be less likely to slip when you are thinking about other things.

ICY TRAILS: In the East during December and, particularly, January there may be little or no snow in the mountains, and rain can turn the concave treadways into sidewalks, slabs and chutes of ice. An easy trail in the summer may become a technical ice climb in January, or even November. When the ground is bare, but temperatures have been below freezing, you should bring your crampons and ice axe. Some people use instep crampons (creepers) in place of full crampons, but these are not much help on steep ice.

Ice can build up to a substantial thickness on top of snow. At one lean-to in Maine my son and I were unable to reach the privy, which was upslope, without wearing crampons. On another occasion I noticed that the moose were walking on top of the snow without breaking the icy crust. On many winter occasions I have seen ice two inches thick on the ledges above timberline and on vertical surfaces that faced the storm.

SLIPPERY GRASS: In the West one sometimes finds grassy (grass or sedge) slopes as steep as 45 degrees (half way from horizontal to vertical). Grass and sedge can become dangerous when made slippery by rain, dew, snow flurries or frost. If you plan to hike on such slopes, you should think in terms of self arrest, and carry an ice axe. You might want crampons.

If you encounter grass or sedge sticking up through ice, do not assume that these tufts will provide traction. The grass or sedge, when lying on the ice under your foot, will be nearly as slippery as the ice.

STREAM CROSSINGS

Occasionally, people do drown attempting a stream crossing while on a hike. Obviously, high water conditions are dangerous. When should you not cross? If you cannot hop from rock to rock, and if the current is so strong that you cannot maintain safe footing even when using a pole to brace yourself, then do not cross. The alternatives are not very attractive, but they are better than drowning. You may be able to go back the way you came. You can bushwhack along the stream, though this may mean going up, over and around steep slopes. You may be able to climb up to a ridge or plateau parallel to the stream where the walking may be significantly easier.

When it rains, streams rise. They are the means by which rainfall, not soaked up by soil, or evaporated, can flow downhill to the oceans. The time that elapses after rainfall starts and when the stream rises will depend on how far it is from the point of interest on the stream to the watershed that received the rain, the slope of the stream, and the amount of rainfall needed to saturate the ground. In the typical mountain setting there is very little soil, even when there is a ground covering of organic matter, trees and shrubs. Stream slopes (gradients) are fairly steep, and the watersheds are close to the point of interest. Consequently streams rise rapidly in the mountains, and they subside relatively quickly, once the rain stops. Even within a few miles of a summit, the watershed may be large. Large watersheds collect lots of water. When the soil can store large amounts of water, the stream can maintain a high flow longer. The watershed without storage will discharge the large amount of water in a short time, so the stream will rise higher. In planning your trip, summer or winter, consider what will happen to the streams you plan to cross in the event of a heavy rain. You should also plan what you would do, if unable to cross.

Streams fed by snowfields or glaciers respond to sunlight when the air temperature is above freezing. What is an easy stream to cross in the morning may be very dangerous in late afternoon. If you plan to return on the same route, you can leave a fixed rope across the stream. The sensible option might be to wait until late at night, when the snowmelt will have subsided, before recrossing the stream. You could wait until the next morning.

Stream crossings in the winter can be very dangerous. Falling through the ice into a swiftly moving stream is likely to result in drowning or fatal hypothermia. It is advisable to cross at a point where you can find rocks under the snow and ice. Often you can determine the location of the rocks by the humps in the ice where the ice has settled over them. Usually it is easier to find the rocks where the stream begins a drop (the water surface goes from nearly horizontal to somewhat steeper).

If heavy rains have washed the stream clear of ice, and subsequent weather has been cold, look for places where "anchor ice" (or bottom ice) has formed below the water surface but on the rocks. Again, you are more likely to find this condition where the stream begins a drop. Here, the anchor ice will build up to the water surface. Though mushy at the surface, anchor ice has good structural strength, as long as the water temperature stays below freezing. See Photo 4-1. Look out for overhanging anchor ice. Probe with your ice axe. Wear crampons.

SNOW AND MUD AVALANCHES

SNOW AVALANCHES: In the Presidential Range of the White Mountains (NH), the U.S. Forest Service maintains a snow avalanche advisory for the safety of winter climbers and skiers. This agency posts at Pinkham Notch daily reports with danger ratings. In other parts of the country, there may or may not be forecasts available. Inquire.

Snow is more likely to avalanche depending on several factors: the rate of snow deposition, type of snow particles, the integrity of underlying snow layers, changes in temperature, the steepness and roughness of the slope, and the time since the snowfall. As snow settles it stabilizes temporarily. Snow crystals begin to change (**metamorphose**) into a more rounded particle shape having less structural connection with adjacent particles. This process can occur more rapidly deep in the snow where heat from the ground may make the temperature higher than it is at the snow surface. To picture the end result of metamorphosis, visualize the upper snow layers resting on a layer of ball bearings.

You cannot tell simply by looking at a slope whether or not it is likely to avalanche. To assess the danger you need information about the layers of the underlying snow as they currently exist (stratigraphy). To obtain this latter information, one must dig a pit down through all the snow layers. One looks for any layer of snow that lacks structure and falls apart.

Rainfall on snow produces a highly dangerous condition, because of the extra weight and the resulting higher temperature in the snow. Also the rain "lubricates" the snow.

Avalanche danger goes up when there is a sudden increase in temperature and/or rain and/or snow fall rates of an inch per hour or more. Avalanches due to snow metamorphosis are less predictable. When temperatures have remained well below freezing for the entire season, the intermediate layers of snow are a little less likely to have metamorphosed to the point of being unstable. Do not make assumptions about the extent to which the bottom layers have metamorphosed.

Some snowstorms begin with gentle winds and snow that has very little of the strength needed to resist one layer sliding over another (shear strength). Subsequent high winds result in hard wind slab snow over the initial snow. The entire slope could avalanche as one slab. As a consequence, it is unwise to hike on hard, sloping snow unless you know what is under the hard layer. One can determine this by digging through the slab. On most hikes you do not have time to dig a proper pit. I recommend that you rely on the U.S. Forest Service experts and their hazard ratings, or local knowledge, where available.

Snow slopes of less than 25 degrees rarely avalanche, and very steep slopes tend to have lots of small sloughs. The existence of closely spaced, mature trees on a slope indicates that avalanche is unlikely, but not impossible. Widely spaced trees provide insufficient support to prevent avalanches. Brush can grow 10 or more feet tall on slopes that avalanche frequently.

MUD AND SNOW AVALANCHES: Spring avalanches are often a combination of mud and snow avalanches. However, it is possible for a steep slope to avalanche (slide) without any snow on it. This is not likely without heavy rainfall. A crucial factor may be the interface in the ground between frozen and unfrozen soil. This surface can be both smooth and highly lubricated by groundwater. Most New England mountains contain sufficient quantities of large boulders to break up such melt surfaces. You cannot tell from looking at a slope where the frostline is in the soil or what the deep soil structure provides in the way of support. Be cautious about hiking on steep terrain in the spring (through June), especially when there are heavy rains.

If you see people caught in an avalanche, try to observe their route and mentally record the last place where you saw them. After the avalanche, post a guard who will watch for further avalanches. Make a quick search for signs of the victim(s). Mark anything that locates the path the victims traveled, and listen for calls for help. Systematically probe the area with whatever you have, for time is important. Rescuers find many victims within 2 feet of the surface.

Send for help when the messenger has full details after the initial search, unless help is very nearby. Be aware that avalanches can deeply bury items in creek bottoms. For more detailed information about snow avalanches see *The ABC Of Avalanche Safety* by LaChapelle.

ROCK SLIDES: The more nearly round fragments of rock are (independent of size) the more easily they will roll. The **angle of repose** (the geologist's term for how steep the pile of rocks, gravel, or sand can be) depends on the particle shape. However, piles of rock undergo weathering and shifting due to freeze-thaw cycles, and what was stable last year may not be this year. You could have a very serious ride down a slope that lets go. A slope made up of uniformly weathered rock, or one with brush growing up through it, is more likely to be stable. Slopes that have recently slid will have rocks showing less weathering than surrounding slopes. Loose rock slopes ending on a glacier are often unstable. Consider suspect lateral and medial moraines on active glaciers even though the moraine slopes are not as steep as the angle of repose. Moraines on an active glacier are moving and distorting, and large boulders may be delicately balanced.

SPRUCE TRAPS

Few beginning winter enthusiasts are aware of the danger of snowshoeing and skiing where the snow is deep around low, closely grown evergreen trees or near timberline. Snow builds up on the branches of softwoods and can bridge across from one tree to another. This can occur without the space under the branches becoming filled with snow. See Figure 4-2, which shows the cross-section of a spruce trap. When the hiker or skier puts weight on these small branches, the branches can bend resulting in the snowshoes or skis going deep into the branches and the space below the snow. The resulting hole may be six feet deep or more. People have even fallen into such holes head first with their snowshoes caught on branches above them. Getting out of this situation alone is very hard work. Work quickly, because you will find that you will become quite wet and cold in short order. If you are caught upside down, you may have to cut your snowshoe bindings to get out, but expedite! Once upright with your snowshoes on, the problem is that of getting one snowshoe off the other and pulling the lower one free. You will probably find that you need to build a snow ramp up out of the hole. You may have to compact snow for some distance before you can get out of the trap. You are unlikely to fall into a spruce trap, if you are on the trail, but the traps may be only a few feet off the trail when the snow is deep.

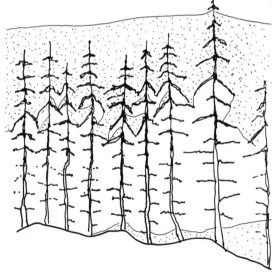

Figure 4-2 Cross Section Of A Spruce Trap

In the West there is a trap that results from solar melting of snow around rocks and trees. Large, deep holes can develop. If, later, wind-driven powder snow fills these holes, the skier or snowshoer may find the front end of his skis or snowshoes unsupported as he or she approaches the tree or rock. It is possible to pitch head first into the soft snow and strike the tree or rock with your head. Be cautious.

WHITEOUT

In winter, reduced visibility caused by fog, snow, or clouds (all of which can move in quickly) and an unbroken snow surface may make differentiation of the snow from fog difficult. Depth perception is also difficult. Particularly, when the cloud cover is thin and the sun brightly illuminates the fog (cloud) from above, the snow on the ground might appear indistinguishable from the fog. Falling snow mixed with fog can be just as hazardous. In any of these situations, you may be unable to detect your approach to a glazed surface, an avalanche slope or the top of a precipice. See Photo 4-2.

Note that fogged glasses and dark are conditions that are the functional equivalents of a whiteout. Either could cause you to not see that you are approaching a precipice or an icy slope.

If the reduced visibility conditions come on suddenly, they may also depart swiftly. Waiting them out might be the best choice. If you must keep going, proceed cautiously. Continue only if you are certain of your position on the mountain. At times, it may be necessary for the first person in line to probe with an ice axe or ski pole to determine what the footing is like ahead. Roping up would be a good idea.

When you will use the same route both to ascend and descend snow slopes, the placement of wands on the way up will help you descend should the visibility decrease. **Wands** are florist's plant supports, bamboo pieces about three feet long and five sixteenths of an inch in diameter. Attach small bits of flagging to the wands. They are usually placed about a rope length apart, but they can be farther apart where the terrain defines the route. Be sure to remove your wands when you descend.

CORNICES

Snow blown across a ridge with steep sides can build up a snow structure that overhangs the steep lee side (the side away from the wind) by 10 feet, 20 feet, or more. We call this a **cornice**. See Figure 4-3. By walking on such an overhanging snow structure you run the risk that the

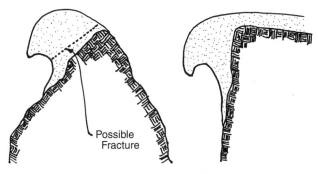

Figure 4-3 - Cross Section Of Cornices

whole thing will collapse, or that you will fall through it. In the latter case, even if you are tied to a companion with a rope, climbing back through the nearly vertical hole in loose snow is not easy. Ideally, you should obtain a look at the ridge from the bottom of the mountain before you climb or from an aerial photograph. Whether or not you can determine the existence of a cornice beforehand, the safer route of travel along a ridge is some distance down the windward side. This might be down where the snow gives way to rock. Do not let the easy walking on top of a cornice beguile you. Note, too, that a flat ridge top can have a cornice, if the lee side is steep.

Though quite rare in the East, it is possible to have a cornice develop in woods that are next to a steep ledge high on a ridge. See Figure 4-4. The resulting snow can be 10 or 20 feet deep and not very dense. While a fall into this snow might not lead to a long plunge, it might be very difficult to get out of the loose snow.

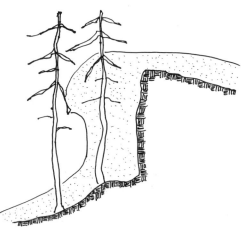

Figure 4-4 - Cross Section Of A Cornice In Woods

CREVASSES AND BERGSCHRUNDS

Ice has substantial strength in compression, but very little strength in tension. As a glacier, which consists of ice, flows over an obstacle and turns corners, the upper surface will crack. These cracks, **crevasses**, can be several hundred feet deep, hundreds of yards long and 20 feet wide or more. There can be many small crevasses (large enough for a person to fall into) all of which become snow covered in the winter. During the spring, the snow bridges over the crevasses will decrease in thickness. As the season progresses, there will be more and more places where a climber can fall through this snow cover. The cover photo shows Mt. Shuksan in late summer. Note that many crevasses are exposed, and the snow covering others is still melting.

Sometimes, it is not possible to tell a glacier from a snow field. The glacier involves snow deep enough to move slowly as a plastic material along its lower regions. If you cannot tell, then assume that there may be crevasses.

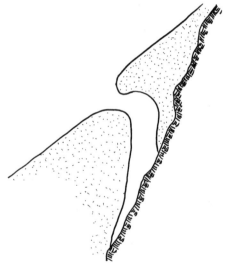

Figure 4-5 - Cross Sections Of A Bergshrund

When a glacier moves downhill, it moves away from the cliff at its upper end and it leaves a gap, like a crevasse, called a **bergschrund**. Technically, a bergschrund is the crevasse and difference in snow elevations that results from the glacier moving away from permanent snow attached to the headwall. See Figure 4-5 above. If there is no snow attached, only a "crevasse" next to the headwall, we call this a **moat**. Crossing from the upper end of a glacier to the headwall can be very challenging, because of the big gap, difference in snow levels, and the possible steep rock face. Often, the moat has a brook or waterfall flowing into it in warm weather. Also, there is likely to be rock fall. The scene might be inhospitable. Early in the season snow might cover the bergschrund. Typically, late in the season, the snow and ice are likely to have receded and the moat or bergschrund will be wider, increasing the problem of crossing.

Large snow fields can also develop deep moats at their uphill ends, particularly late in the summer. This is something to consider when planning to climb or descend steep snow slopes.

ROCKFALL

Roger and I had just crossed below the snout of the Upper Kautz Glacier on Mt. Rainier when I looked back. A rock about 2 feet in diameter bounced and spun down the slope at high speed where we had just crossed. It could have killed either or both of us.

Rockfall is a real hazard on steep terrain. It occurs in the East most commonly in the spring due to the many freeze-thaw cycles that have occurred through the winter. In the West rockfall is common on the higher peaks above the meadows. It occurs randomly, though the likelihood is less when the temperature stays below freezing. For this reason, climbers on high summits in the West make alpine starts (sometime between midnight and dawn) so that they may complete their climb early in the day. As the sun comes up and warms the snow and ice that was preventing rocks from falling, some of those rocks will fall. In some gullies you can hear a constant cascade of little rocks. Note, that rocks fall, so being above them reduces the hazard. If you have a choice, ridges offer greater safety than ravines. The middles of glaciers are often safer from rockfall than the edges, but the crevasse hazard might be greater there. If your route takes you where you could encounter rockfall, then you should expect to make an early start.

Bear in mind that wherever there are steep slopes (steeper than the angle of repose) there is the potential for a rock to fall on you. Rocks fall all summer long, although, for many sites, the probability may be slight. Keep in mind that there is some risk to you and to anyone in your party each time you cross below a steep ledge or cliff. You can minimize the risk by picking dry weather, keeping the time of exposure short, and by choosing alternate routes that do not have as much exposure to rockfall. By looking at the ground below a cliff you may be able to see where rocks have fallen. If you do not see any, the probability of falling rock might be low. You should never consider it nonexistent.

POSTHOLES

Moose tracks in deep snow can leave deep holes! We affectionately call these postholes, and they are a threat to hikers in two ways. First, the hiker who is traveling without snowshoes may step into one of these holes unexpectedly (light, unconsolidated snow might cover the postholes). If the upper layers of the unbroken snow include a hard crust, and the person is traveling rapidly, he or she could break a leg. This is particularly true when traveling downhill. Secondly, if you place a snowshoe on a posthole in such a manner that it is unsupported in the middle, the snowshoe could break. Unfortunately, moose like to walk on trails, which are more open than the rest of the woods. Use caution when you see any sign that a moose, or elk, has been on your trail.

People walking in deep snow without snowshoes can also create postholes. Try to avoid making the trail dangerous for others. People who snowshoe have unkind sentiments toward people who posthole. On the other hand, when the snow surface is so hard that you can walk on it without breaking through, no snowshoes are necessary. Do not leave your snowshoes in the car just because there is little snow, or a crust on the snow, at the trailhead. In the Northeast, you can count on at least three feet of snow in the woods above 4000 feet of elevation by mid March, even though there may be no snow at the trailhead. The hard crust you found at the trailhead may not exist up near the ridge.

ANIMALS

ANIMAL BEHAVIOR: My claim is that animals have feelings and emotions similar to our own. My examples are as follows. On two remote occasions I have seen by the roadside a fox apparently trying to bring its mate or family member back to life. The live fox danced around, and appeared to make quick, unsuccessful attempts to drag the dead mate out of the prone position only to jump back and take more nervous steps. The fox was oblivious to the passing cars. I saw an animal torn by grief and panic. The sight of this animal behavior is heart rending.

My previous cat came to me with an unusually insistent meow. He wanted me to follow him, and he led me to the kitchen where a pot was boiling over on the stove. To me clearly this cat demonstrated concern, and, perhaps, apprehension. I am certainly aware of the moods of my present cat.

Alone one night at Indian Henry's Hunting Ground on Mt. Rainier in 1955, I awoke and saw one of several deer in the moonlit meadow approach me from downwind. When it sniffed the foot of my sleeping bag, it must have been out of curiosity. Deer occasionally follow the tracks of hunters, apparently out of curiosity.

Most female wild animals (and birds) are very protective of their young. It is wise not to get between a cow moose, or a sow bear, and her offspring. We could consider this protective behavior instinctual, or we could say it stems from the same emotions as experienced by protective human mothers.

If you come home to find your dog cowering and submissive, it is a sure bet he has been into some mischief. Clearly the dog understands that you will scold him for the untoward behavior. It seems to me that the dog knows the difference between right and wrong, as seen by humans, and it might be that the dog is demonstrating a conscience and/or remorse.

Any pet owner who has owned a series of pets of the same breed knows that each has a different personality. Any farmer with livestock knows how different their personalities can be. When we have this range of personalities, we should expect to have a few outlaws.

Out of these few anecdotes I cannot prove that animals feel emotions, yet I believe they do.

There are differences in how individual animals react to humans, just as we have a broad range of human response to situations. We can expect great differences in response to our invasion of the home territories of wild animals. Some red squirrels will scold, some come close out of curiosity, and some do both.

You cannot expect wild animals to act in predictable ways. The prior experience of the animal will have a lot to do with how it behaves. Bears wounded by hunters find foraging more difficult, and can become aggressive toward man. You, as an intruder in the territory of the wild animal, do not know what the animal has been through emotionally. You do not have information about its frustrations, health, hunger, territorial interests, social status, parasites, old injuries, mental deficits, or previous interaction with humans.

Animals that become aggressive toward man are equivalent to criminals in that they do not behave in the ways we have come to expect the rest of their brethren to behave. They do not have any respect for you. Because we cannot know ahead of time, it is wise to treat all large animals as potential marauders. Understand that the rogue animal has the equivalent of a gun in terms of the damage it could inflict. It has superior strength (particularly the jaws of the meat eaters), speed and determination.

In the event that an animal bites you, treat the wound as a deep laceration with high probability of infection. Attempt to wash the interior of the wound with large quantities of clean water or disinfectant.

DEALING WITH THE LARGER WILD ANIMALS: There are several defensive strategies one might use to deal with potentially aggressive wild animals:

1) Avoid traveling in known animal habitat, particularly, in the season when young are being protected or during the mating season.

2) You could carry a gun. You would have to have the gun always ready and be mentally prepared to differentiate dangerous behavior. You run some risk of making costly mistakes in the dark, or when you are not calm. You may need a license to carry the gun, and you certainly need to know how to use it effectively. In many parks guns are not allowed.

3) You could carry an aerosol pepper spray can. As long as you do not try to spray the can toward the wind (upwind), you stand a chance of buying some time to retreat. Aggressive animals that have been sprayed may return after a pause in which they regain their eyesight. Private use of such sprays is illegal in some states.

4) Package all food in sufficient layers of plastic so that the smell of the food will not reach your unwanted guests. Similarly, choose food items that are not likely to attract the larger animals. Fish, fried foods and smoked foods are attractants. Any smelly food could make an animal curious. Once you package the food, you should hang it where animals cannot reach it. Do your cooking and washing a long ways from your tent.

5) Prepare yourself with information about the particular species of animals you are likely to encounter on your way to the mountains. For instance, before moose charge they might turn their ears vertically downward beside their heads, so that they look something like water buffalo. They might also raise the fur on the backs of their necks. They can charge without these signs. Seek local knowledge. To not do so is like leaving your map behind on purpose, and

6) Since you mean the animal no harm, why not tell him or her so. Some believe that speaking softly to the animal as you back out of its domain, and avoiding eye contact, is a good tactic. I have no experience here. I certainly would not rely on it, unless you have no other course or you do have a back-up scheme. However, an offensive posture may be effective with some animals in some situations. It worked for me against a black bear at a campground near Dawson, Yukon Territory. I held a paddle up over my head and said in my most aggressive voice, "GO AWAY." The black bear went on its way, continuing to tour the campground looking for easy fare. Note, that this animal was on my turf.

If an animal charges, there is the chance that it is bluffing.

If there is no place to which you can escape, you have run as far as you can, and the attack is one you cannot repel, then you should assume a fetal position that provides the best protection to your vital organs. This will not protect you from the meat eaters.

Be cautious about taking a dog with you. You run some risk that the dog will actually attract the attention of the wild animal. I am thinking primarily of bears. Worse, it could lead the animal back to you as the dog seeks protection. Even the dog's food could be an attractant. If you encounter an aggressive, large animal, then you run the risk of the dog being killed. Unless your dog is trained in how to fight the particular type of large animal you encounter, it would be at a great disadvantage in any confrontation.

SMALL ANIMALS: The smaller animals that often are your enemies include mice, red squirrels, gray squirrels, ground squirrels, picas, marmots, porcupines, and raccoons (a cousin of the bears). These animals will raid your pantry, and eat holes in anything but metal containers. Some will even eat holes in your tent in search of those WONDERFUL salted peanuts (not available in their larder). Some of them will steal your sleep.

Food hung so a bear cannot get to it may still be within the operating territory of a squirrel or other rope climbing species.

Mice, too, will climb and descend a vertical line suspending a food cache. In the East, it is common practice to pass the line that you use to suspend your food through the middle of an empty, clean tuna fish can (open side down with knots in the line on either side). This discourages mice.

Porcupines are very shy, but they are hungry. They will not attack. However, porcupine quills, which could work their way into your body (porcupines sometimes visit shelters), could cause serious consequences. Avoid walking in bare feet. Also, keep in mind that porkies eat boots. If you bring your dog with you, remember that dogs do not know about porcupine quills, which can be fatal to them. So, keep them away from porcupines.

You may find raccoons in campgrounds, but you see fewer of them in the mountains.

BUGS

BLACK FLIES AND MOSQUITOS: It is unwise to underestimate the quantity of insects, their voracity, or the fatigue and hysteria that can result, if you are unprotected overnight in the woods in late spring or early summer. In northern New England the black fly season begins about the middle of May, and is followed by the seasons for no-seeums and mosquitoes. The problem diminishes in August, but bugs are around until September when the frost arrives. The Southeast has chiggers.

Protection from insects includes headnets and insect repellent, if no closed shelter is available. Wood smoke might work. Windy ridges might be bug free.

YELLOW JACKETS: My brother's claim is that he has never been hurt by wild animals or vipers (he spent many weeks in tidewater swamps in Virginia where there are many deadly snakes), but he has been badly treated by yellow jackets, a small, ground dwelling social wasp. These insects sometimes build nests next to trails. While the passage of one hiker might not arouse the nest, the second or third person in a line of hikers is likely to receive the attack. It is not unusual to receive a dozen or more stings.

A bite from a wasp or similar insect could result in anaphylactic shock. This could be fatal, if untreated. Consider carrying the antidote in your first aid kit. Consult your doctor for assistance.

TICKS: Ticks can carry Rocky Mountain spotted fever, which is more common in the Rocky Mountains and the Southeastern U.S. The early symptoms are flu-like. As the illness progresses, there is nausea, vomiting, and abdominal pain. A few days after the first symptoms, a rash appears on the wrists and ankles. If untreated, the illness can be fatal.

Ticks do infect household pets as well as wild animals. A moose can be host to hundreds of ticks, and, in effect, becomes a breeding ground.

Deer ticks, the size of a pin head, can carry a microscopic, coiled bacterium (a spirochete) which results in Lyme disease. The tick bite is usually identified by the concentric ring of rash around the bite. This ring disappears after a few days. Weakness and aching joints can also be symptoms. If you do not obtain treatment, the disease can lead to arthritis and complications similar to those associated with syphilis. This includes general debilitation and permanent damage to the nervous system. While the range of the principal, infected intermediate hosts, mice (particularly, the white footed mouse) and their ticks, is not yet well defined, anyone traveling in grassy areas from late April through October should take precautions. Note, that mice may frequent trail shelters. Also, note that dogs and cattle can carry the ticks and can be infected. It has recently been discovered that deer ticks can carry several other diseases serious to man.

Here are a few precautions you can use to minimize the likelihood of tick bites:

1) Wear light colored clothing including long pants, and tuck your pant legs inside your socks,
2) Use insect repellents with moderate concentrations of DEET (Spray on clothing as well as skin),
3) Avoid wet, grassy areas,
4) Avoid being out during the period when ticks are most active, such as dusk, and
5) Make a careful full-body search each day after being in the field.

By removing embedded ticks within 24 to 48 hours you might avoid infection. To remove a tick grasp as much as you can with tweezers, and pull firmly for as long as it takes. Do not squeeze the tick so hard that it breaks apart. Turning the tick so as to "unscrew" it from your body might facilitate removal.

LIGHTNING

Lightning strikes high peaks. Jim and I were on top of Mt. Teewinot taking each other's pictures on the very pointed summit that is next to the Grand Teton. Clouds began to swirl off the higher peak and Jim insisted we get down off our summit. We did go as fast as we could. When we had descended about 500 feet, lightning did hit the summit. I could feel the surface flow of electricity on the wet rock surface on which I had placed a hand to steady myself.

Lightning can also strike well down in a valley next to a tall mountain. I have seen this occur from a high vantage point. The strike hit a low knob on the lower end of a long ridge of the high mountain I was on at the time. Very intimidating! It is impossible to predict where lightning will strike. On the other hand, lightning is likely to strike more often in high places.

Cloud to cloud lightning occurs even in winter. We believe that lightning is associated with cloud temperatures around freezing.

Lightning is attracted to the highest point in a local area where it is about to strike. That high point makes a better lightning rod, if it is a good conductor. Certainly metal objects are good conductors. Trees, because of the sap in the wood, act as lightning rods. Once the lightning reaches the ground it is again looking for a good conductor. Wet soil and metal well casings act as good conductors. Animals and people are good conductors because of the saline blood in their veins.

Automobiles and dry buildings are the best shelters. If such shelters are not immediately available, reduce your elevation. It is hazardous to stand around above timberline or to continue along a ridge. You could become the equivalent of a lightning rod. If you wonder why metal automobiles are good shelters from lightning, it is because lightning travels on the outer surface of the conductor.

Lightning travels away from the point of strike by following the ground surface, jumping across openings or depressions. Avoid being in any place, such as between boulders or in a cave entrance, where you might become the conductor of the surface (sheet) flow of electricity. Once you stop to wait out the storm, insulate yourself from the ground, by sitting or standing on your non-metallic pack or other dry gear. If you have metallic gear, such as cooking pots, tent poles, stove, or a metal pack frame, do not stay near this gear. Stay away from tall trees. Do not lie down. Separate your party so that you are all at least fifty feet apart. Take this precaution so that if one person is struck there may be someone who can provide first aid. First aid consists of performing CPR, treating for circulatory system shock, and treating for burns.

If you are on ledge that is well below a ridge, you can insulate yourself from possible sheet flow over the ledge by squatting on a separate rock that is on top of the ledge. Usually rock is a good insulator.

Avoid lightning. Heed forecasts predicting "thumpers." Alpine climbers make pre-dawn starts to avoid falling ice in the afternoon. Such early starts should become the norm for avoidance of afternoon thunderstorms on humid days in the summer. If you expect thumpers in the afternoon, then there is no adequate substitute for an early start.

There are many hazards in the wilderness. Think about the hazards and the preparation you might make to meet all of those you could possibly encounter. Sometimes you need skill, sometimes equipment, and sometimes both. Often neither is available on the mountain. Most deserve planning. ❋

EMERGENCY SITUATIONS

The leader should always keep in mind that survival by individual group members depends on many factors, such as stamina, mental attitude, physical conditioning, clothing, experience, good judgment, leadership, and luck. While some can endure unbelievable hardship, others may perish under conditions much less severe. Do not get to that point. Plan well, and make good decisions so that you avoid emergency situations. However, you should be aware of these situations and how to handle them.

This book cannot be a substitute for a first aid course, and I do not cover all possible injuries and treatments. I hope I draw your attention to the fact that your concerns are different when medical help may be days away. Do try to take a wilderness first aid course.

THE LIKELY SITUATIONS

While there are many emergencies that could occur, most common problems fall into the following categories:

SUDDEN BAD WEATHER: You may not see a storm front approaching from the opposite side of the mountain. Above timberline, an extreme change in conditions might suddenly hit you, with rain, wind, temperature drop and low visibility descending on you on very short notice. Should you run down to timberline or stop to dig out your raingear? Each situation will require a different solution, however speed is essential. For this reason, it pays to think ahead as to where your raingear should be in your pack. In some cases, it will help to have a fly or other shelter under which group members may be able to become organized — provided you can persuade enough people to use one hand or foot to hold an edge. It is important for the leader to check that everyone has raingear, not when the rain begins, but at the trailhead.

DARK: Becoming benighted is a situation requiring a decision to proceed, backtrack, or stay put. On most bushwhacks in thickly wooded country, proceeding or retreating in the dark may be out of the question, because of the difficulty of identifying hazards or even the trail itself when you reach it. Generally, travel in the dark is very risky. Retreat on a well-worn trail at lower elevation may be easy, if you have adequate artificial light. It is important that each person have his or her own light. If a light must serve two people, the person holding the light should concentrate on where he or she is stepping, and should be less concerned about where the light falls for the other person. You may point the light in a general direction more beneficial for the other person.

Hiking without a light on a dark night on a snow covered trail may be possible due to reflected light from the snow, but is nearly impossible in the summer. On a smooth trail it is possible to feel your way with your feet. You can greatly facilitate your ability to hike without a light, if you maintain the dark adaptation of your eyes by refraining from turning on any light. However, some people have much better night vision than others. To avoid the necessity of travel at night, you should observe turn around times. Do not become benighted; remember:

THERE IS NO ADEQUATE
SUBSTITUTE FOR AN EARLY START!

INJURIES AND ILLNESS: The third category of mountain emergency situations occurs when there is an accident or illness. Field conditions on a mountain are no better than those experienced by our forebears in their everyday life. In their time, serious injury or illness meant a great danger of dying from infection. You still run that risk, if you do not have on hand appropriate antibiotics and skilled medical care. Lacking either, evacuation becomes of critical importance. In many cases, only hospitals can offer the necessary treatment that the patient must have within a limited time.

ACCIDENT SCENE MANAGEMENT

When someone is injured or ill, the need for first aid may be obvious, but the group dynamics may not be. To prepare for an emergency, have an emergency response plan in mind. In the event of a medical emergency, the leader is expected to assign individual roles. Someone should be in charge of first aid. This means that you or someone in your group should have first aid training. Another looks after the well being of the group members. A third should be in constant communication with the injured person so as to reassure him or her and to obtain information. This last role should not rotate among the party members, because one individual will be more likely to pick up on changes in the patient's condition. Further, the patient will perceive a greater level of care when one person stands constantly by him or her. Of course this does not preclude other party members voicing encouragement.

If the patient cannot walk, then a carry will be necessary. If you suspect spinal injuries, then you should not litter him or her, or even move the person, until you have properly immobilized the injury. This may mean waiting for help to arrive. If you are going to move the injured person, there are several possible methods. On dry, flat ground methods include the fireman's carry (one bearer), the four hand seat (two bearers) and the pole and garment litter (two poles passed through a couple of jackets with two or more bearers). The number of people needed for a litter carry will depend on the length, difficulty and the weight of the victim. In the mountains you will need a party of 12 to 24 litter carriers. Litters are too heavy for people to carry continuously over rough terrain, and, usually, two to four relays of six people are rotated.

I have seen a person with a broken ankle dragged down a snow covered mountain trail by a party of eight people. They used a collection of snowshoes (without crampons) and two poles tied together as a sledge. They met the official rescuers near the base of the trail. The packed trail was too narrow to allow litter carrying. The rescuers brought a plastic toboggan that was much more efficient than the sledge made of snowshoes. We all felt a sense of accomplishment in having brought the patient down in daylight rather than waiting on the mountain for outside assistance.

If you send a party out for assistance, provide them the information about the victim and list of equipment needed. Do not send the party until you gather all the information. Some maps, such as those prepared by the Appalachian Mountain Club, have a rescue information form on the back. You could construct your own form, and carry it with your first aid kit. Five basic kinds of information are needed:

1) <u>A</u>vailable resources at the accident scene (number of people, adequacy of their gear, their suitability as litter carriers, etc.),

2) <u>M</u>edical information relating to the injury, or illness, including an assessment of the victim's overall condition (with vital signs and pre-existing medical condition),

3) <u>P</u>ersonal information about the victim (name, height, weight, age, home address, whom to notify, and tele-phone number),

4) The accurate <u>L</u>ocation, weather, and terrain conditions at the accident site, and

5) The <u>E</u>quipment needed for the rescue (litter, backboard, sleeping bag and any other supplies to prevent further injuries to the victim or other members of the party).

Note that the first letters of the underlined words spell the acronym AMPLE. You should not send the messengers for help until they carry AMPLE information.

I urge every hiker to obtain first aid training. Red Cross courses, Wilderness First Aid training, or Emergency Medical Technician Training are appropriate.

There are hikes above the snow line in marginal conditions where any immobilizing injury could mean death from hypothermia. The leader should be prepared to deal rationally with such a situation. Possible solutions include snow caves, carries, and emergency sledding (including dragging the victim), but, because the remedies must be immediate, you may have to delay sending party members out for help. All uninjured party members must keep physically active until you reach shelter. While I have just suggested that you might have to drag an injured person over the snow, one of the bigger risks to a person with broken bones or other severe injuries is that of dying from an embolism or blood loss caused by movement of the injured parts. **Emboli** are pieces of fat or tissue carried in the circulatory system. When they reach small blood vessels they become blockages that can produce heart attacks and strokes. Immobilize the injured parts (splint the broken bones) before moving the victim to reduce this risk. If the person is in shock, handling him or her roughly by dragging could exacerbate the condition. Do no further harm. Avoid rough handling.

LIFE THREATENING MEDICAL CONDITIONS

HYPOTHERMIA: It is critical that you be prepared to recognize cold hands or ears as the first indication of, potentially, your death from cold. If you are shivering, you are quite cold. The time to do something about it is immediately. To not take action may not only threaten your well being, but may also endanger those with you. Surely you remember how long it takes to warm up from a shivering condition. If you find yourself becoming apathetic, you are lucky to have recognized that you have sunk to level two. There appears to be no way you could recover by yourself from the next stage in hypothermia. Make decisions. Take action.

To give you some idea about how dangerous it is to be cold, consider how little a cup of hot coffee could do for a 160 pound person whose body temperature has dropped by one degree F., the temperature at which serious shivering begins. The coffee has about 1/320th of the mass and heat capacity of the person. As the coffee warms the body and drops in temperature from, say, 137 degrees to 97 degrees, the average body temperature would rise by one eighth of a degree (assuming heat loss from the body has been controlled). The coffee could have been hotter to begin with, but it would be too hot to drink. It takes a lot of hot drinks to warm a truly cold person.

There are several physical processes by which heat can be taken away from the body. If you touch a piece of ice with your skin, the ice rapidly drains heat from your body by **conduction**. If air enters your clothing, warms while cooling you, and flows out the top of the clothing, this cooling is by **convection**. When you feel the heat energy from a bonfire on your face, this heating is by **radiation**. Radiational cooling occurs when the surroundings are much cooler than the exposed skin. If your body and undergarments become wet with sweat, and the air is dry, then the sweat will evaporate, and the body will be cooled by **evaporation**. If you breathe cold air, it has to be warmed to body temperature before you exhale. This process results in cooling by **respiration**.

Both low temperatures and wind bring about chilling by convection. The harder the wind blows against your clothing, the greater will be the cooling. The fast-moving cold front, in addition to providing a drop in temperature, and possibly rain, may turn conditions from calm to a gale in a few minutes! This is what has happened to a hiker caught above timberline by a cold front: He became disoriented with the loss of visibility in the rain or snow. Dressed only for warm conditions, he began to shiver in spite of his physical activity. His strength began to drain away. Scared, he realized that he ought to stop and think, but there was little shelter among the rocks. Soon, his fingers became too numb to open his pack or zip up his jacket, if he could get it on over his arms. Eventually, when he tried to stand up he fell. After coordination was lost, he became irrational. At this point the process became irreversible without outside help. You do not have to freeze to succumb.

We call this condition of lowered body core temperature **hypothermia**. As the body cools down, the circulatory system attempts to keep the core warm by shutting off blood circulation to the outer surface and the extremities. If your feet or hands are cold, you should understand this to mean you are in initial danger of acquiring hypothermia. If you begin to stumble, or your thinking is not very clear, these conditions may be the result of hypothermia. You hope it is not too late to start eating, drinking, seeking shelter and putting on clothes, but it will be soon. In my experience hiking cold (with ears, hands and feet well protected), I have first noticed hypothermia as a sensation of feeling ill with a slight tendency toward nausea. Physical activity and adding clothes have cured me. Sometimes cold hikers will not stop to put on clothes because they do not want the chilling that comes with a stop. It is imperative that you stop to put on clothes when you are cold. Once the clothes are on, resume hiking. If you have already reached your destination, hike uphill a few minutes to regain body warmth.

Conditions that can contribute to hypothermia include injury, illness, use of alcohol, exhaustion, dehydration and, of course, inadequate clothing or sleeping bag insulation. You may be cold throughout the morning because you slept cold. Cool weather alone can bring about hypothermia, but wind and wet clothing speed up the process.

It is important to see that hypothermia is insidious. During an active day, as you run out of energy, your body may cool down past a temperature at which you would shiver, if you were inactive. Being active, you may not notice this cooling. As you warm up, you may be surprised as you go through a long period of shivering. There is a lot of body to warm.

You need to recognize all the clues that you are becoming cold (hypothermic), one of which is stumbling. If you notice that you are not sweating while exercising, be careful to put on more clothes when you stop (and make sure you are not dehydrated). If you do it right away, before you feel colder, you will reduce the risk of hypothermia.

If your feet are cold, put on your hat! The welfare of one part of the body is not divorced from what happens to the remainder. Putting on the hat is important, because a large fraction of your blood circulation goes to your head. The head and neck have about one seventh of the surface area of the body, and it might be essentially bare without that hat! Likewise, putting on wind pants will help keep your feet warm. The cooling of the overall body is reduced, and the warm blood flowing toward the feet is cooled less before it gets to the feet.

If you would like to read a monograph about heat loss and how to keep warm, then I suggest that you read *Secrets Of Warmth* by Hal Weiss.

HYPOTHERMIA TREATMENT: When the condition has not advanced far and the patient is ambulatory, consider descending below timberline or to other nearby shelter before the following steps:

1) Remove wet clothing,
2) Provide warm, dry clothing,
3) Place the victim in a sleeping bag,
4) Put water bottles containing hot water (and wrapped in a garment) in with the victim, and,
5) When he or she is conscious, provide warm drinks.

Try to warm the core (torso) before warming the extremities. If you warm the extremities, the cooled blood flowing towards the core from these outposts might compromise the heart.

If the victim has cooled so far that he or she looks and feels dead, try to maintain body temperature (place the victim in a sleeping bag), and transport the victim to the hospital very gently. A hypothermia victim is not dead until he or she is warm and dead. With a very low body temperature, the victim may still have a very weak, slow, even undetectable pulse, and survive. However, the rewarming process requires sophisticated medical manipulation to be successful.

It is the hiker's responsibility to prevent his own hypothermia. Beginners might not know what to recognize and how to react. It is always the leader's responsibility to monitor the condition of the followers.

Becoming hypothermic is a result of using poor judgment. Plan well, be cautious, be alert, and take action.

MOUNTAIN (ALTITUDE) SICKNESS: The seriousness and complexity of mountain sickness warrant careful study by anyone hiking or climbing above 8-10,000 feet in elevation. Mountain sickness involves cerebral edema and/or high altitude pulmonary edema. Recommended sources of information are *Going Higher* by Charles Houston, *Medicine For Mountaineers*, edited by Wilkerson, and *Mountain Sickness: Prevention, Recognition and Treatment* by Hackett.

The physiological responses of people ascending to altitude vary widely, and can vary in an individual form climb to climb. One or more of the following symptoms of possible mountain sickness might be present: headache, insomnia, lassitude, loss of coordination, edema of the eyes and face, cough, shortness of breath, perceived fullness or tightness in the chest, irregular breathing (especially at night), loss of appetite, nausea, vomiting, reduced urine output, weakness, and legs feeling "heavy" (See Hackett, p. 16).

The treatment for mountain sickness is a descent to a lower altitude, and the administration of oxygen, if available. Treatment should take place before the patient becomes non-ambulatory. People at high altitude who have lassitude, do not eat and drink, stay in their tent, and will not talk might be headed for unconsciousness, a difficult emergency in the mountains.

HEAT STROKE (SUNSTROKE): Initial symptoms are similar to those of heat exhaustion, and include headache, weakness and dizziness. However, this is a life-threatening condition more serious than heat exhaustion. The symptoms differ in that the victim runs a high fever (possibly 106 degrees or more) without sweating. There may be violent vomiting, seizures, and coma due to failure of the body's own cooling mechanism.

First aid involves efforts to rapidly reduce the victim's temperature, usually by means of cold, wet towels applied to the skin. Immediate medical attention is essential. Evacuation should be by litter, and you should handle the victim gently.

As with heat exhaustion consuming large quantities of liquid (3 to 5 quarts per day, or more) and avoiding heavy exercise in very hot weather can reduce the risk of heat stroke. This is particularly true for people who are not in excellent physical condition or who are overweight. A study of Marine Corps recruits at boot camp found that the likelihood of "exertional heat illness" (including heat stroke and heat exhaustion) was related to obesity and to the time it took the recruits to run a mile.[1] With this in mind, be cautious about taking your overweight friends to the mountains on hot days. Even if they are in excellent aerobic condition, they are at greater risk of exertional heat illness, because of the extra load they are carrying.

FRACTURES: As noted above, the most threatening side effect of fractures of the larger bones are pieces of fat or tissue torn loose by the bone ends that enter the blood stream (emboli) and which could cause a stroke or heart attack. The other, and more common, injury is to blood vessels and nerves. If you rupture an artery, whether or not there is external bleeding, you could die from loss of blood. To minimize the likelihood of all of these complications, immobilizing the break is paramount. Major external bleeding and breathing do take priority over broken bones.

Splinting and support of the injury must not interfere with blood circulation. Therefore it is very important to check the pulse beyond the injury during treatment and, at least, every half hour thereafter. Even prior to evacuation swelling could cause a loss of circulation.

RABIES: Skunks, bats and raccoons are carriers of the disease, but domestic pets can also become infected. If bitten by an animal or bat, seek medical help. The disease is fatal without treatment. If possible, bring the carcass of the offending animal in for evaluation, but be careful to handle it in such a way as to avoid being scratched by it.

Recently, a coyote attacked two hikers in New Hampshire. The hikers were able to kill the animal with rocks. The coyote might have been rabid, or it might have been protecting young. Park authorities

---

[1]Gardner, J.W., et al, "Risk Factors Predicting Exertional Heat Illness in Male Marine Corp Recruits," *Medicine And Science In Sports And Exercise*, Mar., 1996.

destroyed the animal before it was tested for rabies. Since rocks are not always available, you might want to carry a ski pole or an ice axe, even in the summer. However it is very, very unlikely that a coyote will attack you.

HANTAVIRUS: After several people died mysteriously, doctors discovered that mice can spread Hantavirus, a respiratory disease that is generally fatal. The doctors believe mouse feces and dust containing the feces can carry the virus. There have not been a great number of cases, and the range of the disease is not well known. It is enough to make one think twice about where one sleeps, particularly after a mouse has run across your face in the dark.

Several other conditions come to mind that could be life-threatening in the mountains where appropriate medical treatment is not available: heart attack, stroke, anaphylactic shock (mentioned in Chapter 4), diabetic shock, and shock from injury. Learn what you can about all these conditions, and provide what help you can. In most cases the only possible means of saving life is through immediate, gentle evacuation.

OTHER SERIOUS CONDITIONS

HEPATITIS: Hepatitis is an inflammation of the liver caused by one of several strains of virus carried by man. The disease can be fatal. Avoid water that, potentially, could have become polluted by human waste. Keep in mind that a trail at higher elevation might cross the stream from which you wish to drink. Water filters might not strain out viruses. See Chapter 12 for suggestions about how to avoid waterborne disease. In general, the chance of a stream being polluted by human or animal waste is greater when there is surface runoff entering streams due to recent rainfall. Because the time of transport in the stream may be long, streams might be polluted for extended periods. Also, note that the lifetimes of microbial vectors are inversely related to temperature. They last longer in the cold. The incubation period is 2 to 6 weeks for one strain of the hepatitis virus and 6 to 26 weeks for another strain. Symptoms include loss of appetite, high fever, and pain in the right upper abdomen. The urine may be dark colored. In today's world, it is best to consider all natural waters potentially polluted. If you are going to drink surface water, then I advise you to treat it. Ask your doctor whether or not you should be vaccinated against hepatitis.

GIARDIASIS: Giardiasis is a disease resulting from ingestion of a water-borne, microscopic parasite. The incubation period is 10 days or so. The symptoms include gastrointestinal distress (burping and diarrhea), lethargy, and weakness. The disease can be fatal for some people in poor health. Beavers, muskrats and birds are thought to be carriers. Man and moose might also be carriers. Since moose are known to spend extended periods of time high on mountains in the winter (including wooded summits), it is possible for streams to be polluted at quite high elevations. To avoid the disease, use a water filter, use iodine pills, or heat the water to at least 160 degrees (F). Since you are unlikely to have a suitable thermometer, bring the water to a boil. This will lessen the risk of other diseases. If you get the symptoms and see a doctor, be sure to ask him if your problem could be giardiasis. The doctor might look for other causes unless he knows you were exposed. See Chapter 12 for suggestions about care in avoiding waterborne disease.

LACERATIONS: The first concern is to stop major bleeding. The second concern is to do whatever you can to minimize the risk of infection, since the trip out to professional care might take several days. Wash wounds as soon as possible with copious amounts of running water and soap or disinfectant. Potable water is fine; it does not have to be sterilized. Bandage in a way that minimizes overall discomfort for the patient. Be sure you do not interfere with blood circulation to the extremities. Check the pulse every half hour. If possible, change the dressings at least daily or when saturated.

FROSTBITE: Freezing increases salinity in tissue cells, which reaches toxic concentrations at -3 degrees C. (27 degrees F.). The distinction, then, between frost nip and freezing which leads to loss of tissue, is this matter of saline toxicity.

Because freezing injures cells, the last thing you want to do is increase the insult by rubbing (even touching) the tissue as it thaws. If the feet freeze and then thaw, the patient must not walk on them. Whether to thaw the feet, or have the victim walk out with frozen feet, is a decision that you must make in the field, and it will depend on the weather, available resources, and the feasibility of evacuation. The victim must not walk so far down the mountain that his or her feet thaw during the hike. There will be significant pain associated with thawing of a frozen extremity.

Frostbite is akin to a severe burn. Infection is a possibility, with consequences that you must not underestimate.

You can avoid frostbite, if you plan carefully and limit what you undertake based on the risk involved.

BURNS: Camping involves use of small stoves, and balancing pots of boiling water on them. Burns from touching the stove (usually minor) and scalds from spilled boiling water are the most common. You can use moist, cool compresses for ten to twenty minutes to provide pain relief. Next cover the burn with burn ointment and a sterile dressing. Severe burns can become infected. When there are severe burns, undertake evacuation.

BLISTERS: Prevention is certainly worth a pound of cure here. To prevent blisters, the hiker must pay attention to his or her feet, and stop when there is any hint of soreness or redness. You can usually accomplish prevention by covering the sore area with adhesive tape. The usual first aid tape will not stick well to damp skin. Some hikers use duct tape because of its tenacious adhesion. Do not put it on over a blister! Removing the tape will take the blister (outer layer of skin) with it. Note, too, that the adhesive chemicals might cause inflammation to sensitive skin. Also, note that tape, or padding material, if it does not stick to the skin, will curl at the edges, will ball up, and might cause more irritation.

If a blister has formed (even an incipient one), treatment involves eliminating the rubbing against the inflamed area. Clean the blister. Place a sterile pad over it, and hold that on with tape. Now, try to reduce the pressure on this injured area. You may be able to accomplish this by placing a donut of adhesive foam padding around the blister. Since this is difficult, it is better to avoid blisters by means of early intervention. Before a hike, some hikers cover with tape those areas of their feet they know are likely to become inflamed. Some hikers use tincture of benzoin as a preventative.

On long expeditions blisters can become infected, leading to serious consequences. Badly infected feet could result in immobilization, and that could lead to a struggle for survival.

Note that boots can rub and cause blisters either from being too loose or from being too tight. If the boots are loose, consider adding more socks or another layer of inner sole to help fill the boot. If the boots are too tight, remove these items. If the boots press on a particular spot on the foot, add adhesive foam padding around that spot on the boot. A thin liner sock can reduce rubbing.

SNOW BLINDNESS: Exposure to prolonged bright light can result in a very painful condition called snow blindness, a hazard to anyone who travels on snow. The patient's eyes feel as if they have gravel in them, and are extremely painful. Any bright light induces pain. In severe cases, temporary blindness occurs, which might last for a couple of days.

To avoid snow blindness you must limit the amount of light that enters the eyes. Dark glasses with light-shields on the side (glacier goggles) are the appropriate eye protection. The Indians of the arctic use(d) goggles made of wood or bone with just a narrow slit out of which they can see. In a pinch, you might be able to jury rig something similar, such as a piece of cardboard with small holes through which you can see. The alternative is not very attractive; it can be excruciatingly painful.

UV HAZARD AND SUNBURN: Above timberline and in open country there is no shade. You are constantly exposed to ultra violet (UV) rays during the day. On snow or ice the situation is worse, because of the reflected rays. The UV exposure is greater at altitude, because of the reduced amount of atmospheric absorption and scattering. The rays can result in sunburn, skin cancer (over the long run), and the early onset of cataracts. Beginners are inclined to underestimate the amount of exposure that they might receive on snow.

To avoid sunburn, I recommend that you wear a long sleeved shirt, long pants, a visored cap (or, preferably, a broad brimmed hat), sunscreen on your ears, neck, face and hands, and under the chin. Provide UV protection for your eyes.

If you become badly sunburned, it is very important to avoid further abuse by solar rays or physical bruising. First aid involves application of sunscreen to prevent further assault, and, in severe cases, application of a burn ointment and cold compresses where there is swelling. Aspirin is recommended for pain relief. Drinking tea is also found to be beneficial, and a compress made from tea bags may provide relief.

Some people burn badly on their lips. This can become quite serious, if not treated right away. Prevention involves coating the lips with zinc oxide ointment or lip balm with a substantial solar protection factor (SPF).

DEHYDRATION: If you allow your body to dehydrate, your blood becomes thicker (more viscous) and does not flow as easily. Symptoms can include loss of energy and/or a loss of a sense of well-being (malaise). When the blood is thick, heat and energy-providing glycogen are not distributed to the muscles where needed. Loss of energy and frostbite can result in cold weather. In hot weather the thicker blood does not do an efficient job of carrying waste heat to the skin, and hyperthermia (heat exhaustion or heat stroke) might result. Other conditions brought on by dehydration include fatigue, abdominal or leg cramps, headache, and dizziness. Dehydration is considered a medical emergency and can be fatal.

Dehydration can sneak up on you, particularly in a dry, cold climate. When the air temperature is low the air has to be heated by the lungs to body temperature. Heating of air reduces its humidity. If you start with cool, dry air it will be very dry air when warmed in the body. The body has to add moisture to the air so that the lungs will not dry. You can lose a lot of water as respired moisture when working hard in cold weather.

You should drink two or more liters of water during a strenuous hiking day, and *at least* another liter when you camp for the night. Often a water deficit of two liters or more develops during a strenuous hiking day, in spite of what seems like adequate intake during the day. For some people drinking a lot in the evening keeps them awake. Be sure your intake is adequate, since sleeplessness can result from dehydration. You tend to dry out overnight, so be sure to drink a lot at breakfast. Athletes have found that it is much easier to consume and adsorb adequate water that is lukewarm than it is to take in that much volume of cold or hot drinks. Have your hot drinks, but be sure the total intake is adequate.

People who have long bouts with vomiting and/or diarrhea can lose a lot of liquid. Sometimes they are unable to keep down whatever they drink. If they become dehydrated enough, they will become unresponsive. Since you cannot ask an unresponsive person to drink, that person is in a very tenuous situation. Do not force drinking. Choking or even drowning could result. In a hospital saline solution is given intravenously, and usually the patient soon revives. In the field, that is not an option for most groups. Even with hospital treatment there is significant mortality among people who become this dehydrated. Do not go hiking with anyone who has a stomach bug or when there is any hint that anyone in your party could fall victim to vomiting or diarrhea.

LEG CRAMPS: Most people can hike without leg cramps. I consider leg cramps a serious issue because I have heard of a case in which the victim passed out while hiking when under the influence of severe cramps in both legs. The potential injury from a fall while unconscious is the serious risk. Some people are severely debilitated by this affliction, usually after the hike or during the night. Stretching helps prevent cramps. Quinine sulfate is effective as a cramp preventative for some people. Just drinking lots of water may prevent or relieve cramps, and it is the recommended treatment

Taking an "electrolyte replacement," such as Gatorade®, may prevent or relieve leg cramps. Increased potassium may help. Taking table salt is thought to help, but does not address the underlying cause, inadequate flushing of the lactic acid debris in muscles. Salt intake results in further dehydration of the system. So, salt should be taken sparingly and with lots of water. I have found that I can get rid of or avoid leg cramps by adding an extra layer over the lower part of my body at night to keep it warmer. Massaging the cramped muscle may help; do it so as to encourage circulation toward the body core.

HEAT EXHAUSTION (PROSTRATION): When the body's cooling system is overworked, dehydration results along with a decrease in circulation. There may be headache, dizziness, weakness and stupor. The skin becomes pale and clammy. First aid involves having the victim lie down in a cool place and the victim drinking lots of cool liquid. Loosen clothing. Seek medical treatment if the victim does not respond to field treatment.

In hot weather, particularly in hot, humid weather, it is prudent to drink plenty of liquid and avoid heavy exercise in order to reduce the risk of heat exhaustion.

Prepare for emergencies. Learn first aid. Think through what you would do in the event of any possible accident or illness that might occur to anyone in your party, including yourself. It is not a matter of being a hero; it is part of the contract you have with your partners. When an emergency occurs, take action. Look after everyone. Assign roles. Use every resource. ❋

MOUNTAIN WEATHER

On a mountain the weather is often an important factor leading to extreme discomfort, injury, and death. We want to identify the types of weather that are dangerous, the elements of mountain weather, and how to make or obtain weather forecasts.

DANGEROUS MOUNTAIN WEATHER

COLD FRONTS AND SQUALL LINES: Cold fronts and squall lines are dangerous because they can bring with them an abrupt increase in wind (up to hurricane force), a quick drop in temperature, and sudden, heavy rain. They also bring reduced visibility and possible thunderstorms. This is the classic weather change that can result in hypothermia, and it can arrive in the middle of the night without warning.

A **squall line** is a long line of turbulent weather advancing more or less perpendicular to the line, and providing a rapid change to windy, rainy conditions (a squall). Squalls are thought of as brief events, but the rain and wind, though reduced, can continue for several hours. Squall lines can be terrifying with black sky and, possibly, lightning along the front from horizon to horizon. Ominous, still air usually precedes the squall line. You should be afraid. The ensuing wind and rain can do dreadful damage. Squall lines are a summer, humid air phenomenon. They usually precede cold fronts. Tornados can be generated by the turbulence in a squall line.

Cold fronts are an air mass phenomenon; they are associated with low pressure circulating air mass systems. They appear similar to squall lines in that you may see the approach of a line of dark clouds. Often, it is already raining when the cold front arrives. The wind and rain usually increase, and there may be lightning. A dramatic shift in wind direction and temperature is often apparent.

Cold fronts are particularly hazardous to the person hiking in the fall. At that time of year hikers are often not prepared for winter conditions. Whenever you are hiking, consider what a 20 degree temperature drop and high wind could bring. In the fall it is not uncommon to hike at a temperature below 50 degrees, so a 20 degree drop would result in below freezing conditions! Always check the forecast. Use good judgment. Try to stay dry. Be prepared.

RAIN, SNOW AND FOG: Rain in the winter or snow in the summer can get you into big trouble. These can arrive slowly with a "warm" front, so that you have 6 to 24 hours warning from the sequence of conditions that provide increasing cloudiness. If you are several days walk from the trailhead, you may be in for a bad time. When your clothes become wet, they lose most of their insulating value, perhaps, just before a cold front arrives. Becoming wet by snow in the summer, when you are unprepared for such conditions, is also an invitation to terminal hypothermia. Any rain near freezing and freezing rain are extremely dangerous to the person without substantial shelter.

Fog, which can occur anytime of year, can wet anything in its path. Leave the door open to your tent, and everything in the tent might become quite wet by morning. This is particularly true, if the tent faces into the wind. Walking in fog can make you as wet as if it had rained. The most common type of fog seen by hikers is "up-slope fog," which forms as moist air sweeps up the side of a mountain. As the air cools, the moisture condenses to form an "orographic" cloud (fog) at upper elevations of the mountain.

Unexpected fog (cloud) or blowing snow can ruin your day, if you lose your bearings and cannot proceed or retreat. Contemplate the combination of loss of bearings and rain at a temperature near freezing next time you are seated beside a warm fireplace.

HOT WEATHER: Clear, hot weather in the mountains can threaten your health through dehydration, sunburn, heat exhaustion or heat stroke. Hot, dry weather increases the loss of moisture from the body by evaporation. The resulting dehydration reduces the ability of the body's cooling mechanism to get rid of excess heat by evaporation. Similarly, hot, humid conditions are a great danger to the body working hard, because the high humidity reduces the possibility of cooling the skin by evaporation of sweat. The heat buildup in the body can be fatal.

THUNDERSTORMS: Thunderstorms can deliver torrential rain, high winds, and lightning. They are an example of well-channeled vertical circulation in which moist, warm air rises, and then releases rain and heat. If more moisture vapor is available, additional heat energy can fuel further rising air. A thunderstorm cell is this vertical circulation of moist air that results in static charge separation and the development of lightning. Thunderstorm cells have limited lifetimes, because they have limited supplies of moisture. New cells can form next to the old ones. When air is forced up over a mountain, the vertical movement can create a thunderstorm right over the peak. This thunderstorm formation can occur without the warning you normally have. Usually you can see (See Photo 6-1.) or hear a storm coming. The only warning you might have on the mountain could be when the sky becomes very dark and ominous.

Thunderstorms can accompany squall lines and cold fronts where the contrast between the adjacent cold and warm air masses results in the strong upward movement of the warm air. Local thunderstorms usually form in the afternoon. Humid conditions precede them. Often, hazy skies limit the visibility to under a mile, obscuring the approach of a thunderstorm. If afternoon thunderstorms are in the forecast, then it is wise to be off the mountain by noon.

To accomplish this, start your hike early. Make an alpine start. As mentioned in Chapter 4, alpine climbers start before dawn to avoid the ice and rock fall that occur after the sun warms the environment.

THERE IS NO ADEQUATE
SUBSTITUTE FOR AN EARLY START!

MOUNTAIN WEATHER CONDITIONS: Conditions on the upper portions of a mountain can be more severe than they are at the base of the mountain for the following reasons:

1) The higher you go the colder it gets, except on still, clear nights when inversions occur,
2) As the air cools going up the side of a mountain, the relative humidity becomes higher. If 100% humidity is reached, cloud (up-slope fog) and, possibly, precipitation will be produced at higher elevation,
3) The visibility might be severely limited by the fog,
4) The winds are stronger on the upper parts of a mountain,
5) The terrain will be more exposed to the weather than it would be below timberline, and
6) Very moist air moving up the side of a mountain can result in the development of a thunderstorm cell over the peak with no advanced warning other than a dark cloud overhead.

All of these conditions can occur *without* a storm.

If you want to know more about weather, but find big words and obscure concepts difficult, probably the most useful document for you is a book full of pictures showing the various types of clouds and associated forecasts. See *Instant Weather Forecasting* by Alan Watts. Note that Mr. Watt's forecasting guides are useful, even when you know more about weather.

THE ELEMENTS OF MOUNTAIN WEATHER

COOLING-WITH-ALTITUDE: When air sweeps up the side of a mountain and expands in response to the lower pressure with increasing altitude, the air cools. The air usually does not pick up thermal energy, and the process is called **adiabatic expansion.** I will refer to it as cooling-with-altitude. The amount of cooling of the air as it rises (the adiabatic lapse rate) is about 5.5 degrees Fahrenheit per 1000 feet of elevation gain in air not saturated with moisture vapor. This assumes that the wind is blowing and the air moves up the side of the mountain. The wind blows around mountains as well as over them, the sun warms the air as we climb, and other factors complicate the cooling-with-altitude picture.

While the actual conditions on the mountain might not show a linear change in temperature with altitude, the difference in temperature from the bottom to the top will generally average about 3.5 to 4 degrees per 1000 feet. If the air reaches the dew point as it cools while ascending, above this altitude the cooling-with-altitude rate will be as little as 3.25 degrees F. per 1000 feet.

I want to emphasize that when the wind blows it is colder as you go to higher altitude. As an example, the *highest* recorded air temperature on top of Mt. Washington[1] (NH) is 72 degrees F., which occurred on a day when the valley probably had a temperature over 100 degrees.

If the temperature was 45 degrees at a trailhead at 2000 feet on Mt. Washington, the temperature on top might be 28 degrees (with blowing snow). On a 14,000 foot peak with a 7000 foot high trailhead the temperature difference could be as much as thirty-five degrees.

It should be pointed out that if you start up a mountain when there is an inversion and no wind, you might climb above the inversion or the inversion might be quickly blown away.

INVERSION CONDITIONS: On clear nights after the wind dies, near the ground air loses heat by radiation to space and at a slower rate upwards as high as one or two thousand feet above the ground. By the middle of the night, and until sunrise, temperatures are lowest near low terrain, and increase upward. This fairly common condition is referred to as an "inversion of temperature."

In an inversion the temperature increases as one goes up in altitude — up to a point. At the top of the inversion layer there will be an abrupt discontinuity in the slope of the temperature profile. Below this point inversion conditions apply. Above this point the temperature decreases with altitude. Smoke and smog can rise as high as the top of the inversion layer, but are trapped by the colder, denser air above. See Photo 6-2. Note carefully that inversion conditions do not occur when the wind is blowing. Wind usually disperses an inversion layer.

Often inversion layers trap moisture as valley fog (cloud layer). This can be impressive when seen from above as an "undercast."

---

[1]Mt. Washington is 6288 feet high, the home of "the worst weather in America," and where an observatory has been maintained for most of the time since 1932. It was here that the highest recorded surface wind speed was measured — 231 mph.

On still winter nights, when the valleys might experience temperatures around thirty below, it may be as much as thirty degrees warmer high on the mountain. When we receive a high speed delivery of cold, Canadian air, the reverse might be true. Because still conditions are less frequent than windy conditions, you should plan on the latter.

MOUNTAIN WINDS: When an inversion forms on a still night over hilly or mountainous terrain, warm air rises and cold air sinks. There can be a down-slope breeze in the evening, which can be particularly strong in steep canyons. Correspondingly there can be an up-slope breeze in the morning after the sun is up.

The weather conditions on top of a mountain include winds that are stronger than those found near the base of the mountain. Winds at high altitude above ground are stronger, because there is less influence of friction with the ground surface. This helps to account for high winds on isolated peaks. A second factor contributing to higher winds at altitude is that air forced to move upward and over a mountain is squeezed toward the top of the atmosphere, and must move faster in order for a given volume of air to go through the smaller cross section. In effect, the air goes through a bottle neck. See Figure 6-1. Peaks, ridges and passes, or cols, might become much windier than the ravines below. I have seen eastern white pine trees with the bark ground off their small branches by wind driven ice pellets. This was in a very limited region at the end of a ridge in Vermont.

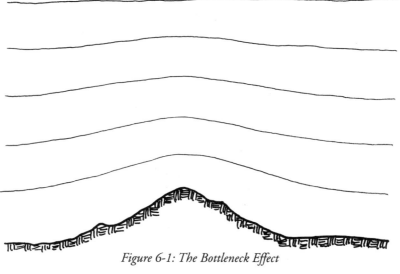

Figure 6-1: The Bottleneck Effect

CONDENSATION: You have seen dew form on the side of a glass of cold drink in the summer and on eye glasses when you come into a warm room from the winter cold. If the eye glasses are at a temperature well below freezing, the result would be frost (ice crystals) instead of dew. The cold glass, and the eyeglasses, are at temperatures lower than the respective dew points. The **dew point** is the temperature at which condensation (dew, fog, cloud, or frost) would form, if the air were cooled. At 100% humidity the dew point (temperature) and the air temperature are the same, and the air contains all the moisture it can hold. The more moisture in the air the closer the dew point will be to the air temperature. The warmer the air is the more moisture it can hold; as air is warmed without moisture input, the humidity decreases. When air cools the humidity increases.

Note that as the air cools down in the evening, the air temperature approaches the dew point, and dew might result. When the temperature rises in the morning, the dew point is not going to change much, particularly if the wind is not blowing. If a different, moister air mass moves in, or the sun evaporates moisture from trees or bodies of water, the dew point will rise. If you camp on a valley floor on a still night, where the temperature might well become colder, there is a good chance of dew forming on your tent and your gear left outside.

Remember that the dew point is the temperature at which condensation (dew, fog, cloud, or frost) would form, if the air were cooled.

HEAT ENERGY OF CONDENSATION AND OF EVAPORATION: It takes a significant amount of energy to free (evaporate) molecules of water from a droplet of fog or to change liquid droplets, which you see as fog, to the gaseous phase, which you cannot see. As part of a drop of rain evaporates, the drop is cooled, and so is the surrounding air. The opposite effect occurs when droplets form from the invisible vapor in the air; heat is given up to the droplet and surrounding air. The air warms. I am talking about a big deal here. Lots of energy is involved.

Now, I have said that, when evaporation takes place, cooling occurs. That is true when there is no input of energy to the system (air and the moisture it carries). However, solar energy can drive evaporation. The input of solar energy can both warm the air (separating the air temperature from the dew point) and provide the energy of evaporation needed to turn condensation (fog) into invisible moisture vapor. This happens when solar energy "burns off" the morning fog.

When rain begins, its evaporation near the earth's surface can result in a temporary, noticeable cooling of the air. Once the rain has fallen heavily for awhile, the air temperature near the ground will become very close to that of the air from which the rain fell. That air will be several thousand feet higher and correspondingly cooler. So you should expect cooling when rain begins.

INSTABILITY: Instability refers to the condition in which some air at a particular altitude is warmer than other air at the same altitude. The warm air will rise, and it will cool as it does so. If it does not cool enough to become stable, with the same temperature as the surrounding air, it will continue to rise. If the rising air contains much moisture vapor, as it cools to the dew point, cloud will form. As cloud droplets form, the release of the heat of vaporization warms the air in which the droplet is immersed. This air expands and is buoyant. It rises with respect to the surrounding air that does not have cloud. As the air rises it cools causing more cloud to form and the generation of more heat. As long as there is more moisture available, the process can continue. That is how thunderstorms form.

THUNDERSTORMS: When the surrounding air for thousands of vertical feet is colder than the rising air that is condensing moisture, the vertical development of clouds can continue to heights as great as 50,000 or 60,000 feet. These clouds of rising air are congested cumulus or cumulonimbus or thunderstorm clouds. When they rise to great heights they will have an upper portion composed of ice crystals, the anvil top (See Photo 6-1). Congested cumulus clouds can produce showers or heavy showers, sometimes hail and strong wind, but no lightning. Cumulonimbus clouds produce thunderstorms of varying intensity, depending on how high the tops are.

Thunderstorms occur as isolated events on humid afternoons. They also occur with air mass systems in squall lines and with cold fronts, which can reach you at any time of night or day. In the case of squall lines, the whole mountain range becomes exposed to lightning, and the possibility of ferocious winds, dramatic drops in temperature and torrential rains. Watch those forecasts. If you are out for several days, and do not receive weather forecasts, beware of dark clouds covering the horizon.

MOUNTAIN-INDUCED PRECIPITATION AND RAIN SHADOWS:
Mountain (orographic) weather is a term that includes the phenomenon
of the cloud at the top of a mountain. If the mountain is high enough
and if the air is sufficiently moist, then the **orographic** (mountain in-
duced) cooling of the air will result in precipitation high on the mountain.

You might wonder why the orographic cloud, once formed, does not
flow down the far side of the mountain. Just as the air cools as it flows up
to higher altitude, it also warms when descending to lower altitude and
higher atmospheric pressure. If precipitation falls on top of the mountain,
the air will be drier on the second side of the mountain than it was on the
first side. "Rain shadows" are places where less than average precipitation
occurs, because there is little moisture in the air they receive. The area
northeast of the Olympic Range in Washington State is an example
(particularly the San Juan Islands). The average annual precipitation is
quite low there. Similarly, the plains and valleys east of the Sierra Nevada
Mountains in California, and those east of the Cascade Range in Washington and Oregon, are much drier than the country between these
mountain ranges and the Pacific ocean. The bulk of the weather in those
states moves east from the Pacific Ocean. Much of the moisture contained in the weather systems moving off the ocean is lost as precipitation
in the coast range of mountains where there is higher than average precipitation. In the East the valleys east of the Appalachian Mountains
receive less precipitation than the peaks. Even a thousand feet of elevation difference can affect the amount of precipitation.

FORECASTING WEATHER

The science of weather prediction has not overcome the
unpredictability of weather. In your ventures out beyond touch with
civilization (weather radios and TV weather channels) you must hedge
your bets. Even the forecast you heard two days ago might be very
wrong. Be particularly careful to note that the common weather forecast
is aimed at folks who live in the lowlands. Conditions in the mountains
are generally cooler, cloudier, windier, and wetter (snowier).

Photo 6-3 shows what are called fair weather cumulus clouds. The
dew point and air temperature are the same at the elevation of the

bottoms of the clouds. Instability accounts for the turbulent upward movement in the cloud. The fact that the clouds do not continue growing taller indicates that there is insufficient moisture to support this development. On those days when such clouds form, commonly the day will start clear. As the sun evaporates moisture from the trees and water, these clouds begin to form. As the day progresses, the percentage of sky coverage increases. So long as the clouds do not reach great altitudes in their vertical development, no thunderstorms will occur. When more humid air is available, thunderstorms may occur. When the day starts with cumulus clouds already covering much of the sky, the indication is that there is much more humid air aloft, and showers are possible.

The cumulus clouds often quickly dissipate as the sun starts to set. Do you wonder why the clouds dissipate at a time when the air cools? When the heat energy source and evaporated moisture are shut off, the clouds evaporate into surrounding, drier air, or are replaced by drier air.

Notice that in Photo 6-3 there is a thin layer of clouds at a much higher altitude. This cloud layer may be part of a warm front, a topic discussed later.

WEATHER SYSTEMS: The progression of high pressure and low pressure circulating systems characterizes global weather. In the temperate zone (most of the U.S. and Canada) these systems generally move from west to east around the globe. The direction of travel is determined by jet streams in the stratosphere, stationary highs (like the Bermuda High established in the summer), ocean currents and trade winds. While we usually think in terms of lows and highs as circulating air masses (meteorologists call these cyclones and anticyclones, respectively), lows and highs can exist as troughs and ridges of atmospheric pressure. When a stationary low pressure trough occurs, we often have a series of low pressure cells moving along the trough, each with its inclement weather, but with no real clearing in between these events.

AIR CIRCULATION AROUND HIGHS AND LOWS: Air moves from high pressure systems towards low pressure systems. You might wonder why air does not just rush in to fill a low pressure zone and make a big bang when the low is filled. Any object on the surface of the globe is moving in a circular path around the axis of the earth as the earth turns. A moving object free of contact with the earth, such as a bullet or air propelled in wind, goes in a deflected path. In the Northern Hemisphere that path is somewhat to the right of where one would think it should go. In the Southern Hemisphere moving objects swerve to the left. This effect (the Coriolis Effect) is caused by the fact that the earth is turning under the moving object. Air flowing toward a low pressure zone north of the Equator swerves to the right, and the winds appear as a counterclockwise circulation as seen from above. See Figure 6-3 in which the arrows show the direction and relative speed of the wind. Similarly, air moving away from a high pressure system turns to the right and the high pressure cell has clockwise circulation, as seen from above.

Winds near the surface of the earth are a continuum of air movement from higher to lower pressure. The greater the difference in pressure and the closer the high and low are, the higher the wind speed will be.

You can estimate in which directions a center of low pressure and a center of high pressure are from you. When you face the wind, the low pressure is to your right and somewhat behind you. The high pressure center is to your left and somewhat ahead of you. This does not tell you in what direction the low or high is moving, but you should know the direction in which these usually move in your part of the country

Above I explained why the winds blow in the directions they do, but note that the central region of a low pressure system contains air that is moving upward to higher altitude. See Figure 6-2. Conversely, a high pressure system contains a central region with cold, descending air.

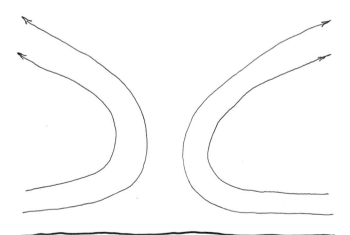

Figure 6-2: Schematic Vertical Cross Section Of A Low Pressure System

Figure 6-3 shows a schematic representation of a low pressure system from above (in plan view). There are two fronts reaching out from the center. Both fronts are progressing counterclockwise around the low. The **warm front**, which is made up of moist, warm air riding up over somewhat cooler air, is designated by solid half circles on the front side

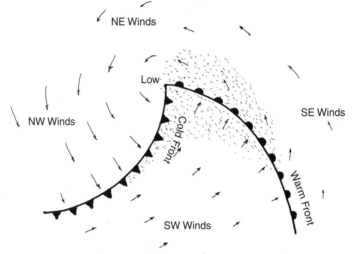

Figure 6-3: Schematic Plan View Of A Low Pressure System

of the line indicating its location. In a **cold front** dense, cold air pushes away warmer air. Cold fronts are designated by solid triangles on the front side. A cold front moves faster than a warm front, and it can catch up to the warm front. In that case we have an **occluded front** shown by alternating half circles and triangles on the front side. See Figure 6-4.

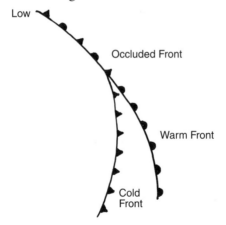

Figure 6-4: Schematic Plan View Of An Occluded Front

Also note the direction of wind flow shown by little arrows in Figure 6-3. Note that there is a shift of as much as 90 degrees or more in wind direction from one side of the cold front to the other. If you are northeast of the storm, which way would the wind be blowing?

Figures 6-5 and 6-6 show a low pressure system at two locations as it progresses northeast across New England. Imagine that you are at Monpelier, VT. You would experience first southeast winds, then northeast, north and northwest winds.

Figure 6-5: Schematic Plan View Of A Low Pressure System Located At Albany, NY

The winds would **back** or the compass direction from which they come would decrease. If you were at Boston, MA, you would experience southeast winds, southwest winds after the warm front, and northwest winds after the cold front. The winds would **veer** or the compass direction from which they come would increase. You might be far enough from the storm path that the cold front passage would be a very moderate shift in wind direction and without violent weather. If you were in Concord, NH, you would experience a rather quick shift from southeast winds to north or northwest winds as the low passed.

It is possible to predict this progression of events at a given location, if you know the path of the low pressure system. Similarly, if you have seen most of the events, you can predict what will follow. However, not all systems are as simple as described above. Stationary fronts can cause rain for a week. On rare occasions lows can move northwest instead of east to west. Normally, when the wind shifts into the northwest you can be sure that you will experience much improved weather, at least for a day or so. Fine days can also occur without the precursor low.

Figure 6-6: Schematic Plan View Of A Low Pressure System Located At Portland, ME

FRONTAL CROSS SECTIONS: Figure 6-7 shows the schematic cross-section of warm front weather. As a warm front approaches you, the clouds will change from a clear sky, to mares' tails or other high wispy cirrus clouds. See Photo 6-4. Note that when thin wisps of clouds are bent it represents the influence of wind at two different altitudes blowing in different directions. Next in the sequence will be a high, thin, hazy cloud grading into a high overcast (Cirrostratus, see Photo 6-5), followed by stratified clouds at intermediate height (Altostratus, see Photo 6-6) and lower stratified clouds (Stratus, see Photo 6-7). Finally there will be stratified clouds with rain or snow (Nimbostratus clouds). Stratified clouds are layers of cloud without puffiness. It may take from six to twenty-four hours for the progression of events to occur. The whole sequence is referred to as the warm front. The lower the clouds, the closer you are to receiving precipitation. Often, there are only light winds as a warm front approaches. The strength of the wind is an indication of how energetic the low might be. Sometimes, there are puffy clouds below the stratus clouds resulting from unstable air at altitudes below the warm front. While the specific clouds you observe in an advancing warm front may vary from simple, stratified form, you should be looking for a sequence of lowering, stratified clouds.

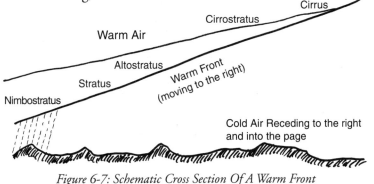

Figure 6-7: Schematic Cross Section Of A Warm Front

Figure 6-8 shows a cross-section of a cold front. While warm fronts are usually not accompanied by turbulence and thunderstorms (the warm air rides up over the cold air), cold fronts involve a more dramatic pushing of warm air aside by blustery, cold winds. Thunderstorms might occur before the frontal passage, or after it, but the greatest likelihood of turbulent conditions is when the front comes through your area. At that time warm, moist air comes in contact with cold air, the warm air rises, and precipitation occurs.

Figure 6-8 — Schematic Cross Section Of A Cold Front

Figure 6-9 shows the schematic cross section of an advancing (nonstationary) occluded front. Such fronts can hide the vigorous nature of the cold front in the advancing, placid warm front.

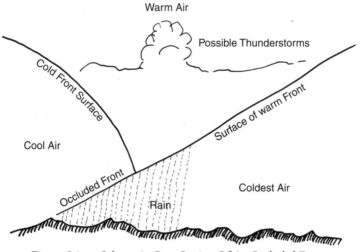

Figure 6-9 — Schematic Cross Section Of An Occluded Front

RAINY SEGMENTS: Rainy, snow, and showery weather are most prevalent in the area north through east from a warm front. Behind the cold front there may be brief showers or snow flurries, but the air becomes progressively drier. The heaviest rains usually precede the passage of the warm front at ground level, and accompany, more briefly, the passage of the cold front. Sometimes, we have a "clearing off" shower as a mild cold front comes through the area.

PREDICTING WEATHER: As mentioned in the section on WEATHER SYSTEMS above, there are many weather sequence possibilities. When we have a progression of highs and lows, you can predict what will happen. You can even guess that there is a good possibility that a warm front will follow the clear day you are experiencing. In New England we call those clear days "weatha breedas." The next day, the day during which the warm front progresses towards you, can be a great hiking day. It may be clouding up, however the winds are often light, and the temperature will be moderate. You must be off the mountain that day, or be prepared for storm conditions!

The first twenty-four hours after a cold front can be the clearest air you will experience, even though there may be some lingering clouds. After the air becomes clear, it will begin to become hazy.

If you experience a warm front approaching, note which way the wind is blowing. Is it veering, or changing in a clockwise manner? It would change from the south to southwest to west as the low passes north of you. Is it backing, or changing in a counter-clockwise way? It would change from the south to the southeast to the east indicating that the low will pass south of you.

If the day after the passage of a low, and its cold front, is cloudy instead of clear, do you have a stationary system, or is there another low following on the heels of the first? You might be able to distinguish these two possibilities by looking for the progression of warm front conditions.

Weather prediction is something you can practice at home. Observe the cloud type and sequence, and the wind direction. Keeping track of what happens each day and how it relates to the next day's weather will give you the perspective to predict what will happen tomorrow based on what is happening today. Are the current conditions characteristic of a warm front? Is the wind in the process of shifting into the northwest? What is your guess as to tomorrow's weather?

To avoid dangerous conditions, pick your weather carefully. You may want to optimize the weather for hiking by traveling to the mountain on the day that you expect the weather to clear.

Local experts can tell you which season of the year has the least inclement weather. However, patterns of less desirable weather settle in for long periods. They are dependent on the existence of stationary high pressure areas farther east.

If you are on a mountain in a rainy spell of some duration, you may have to decide whether to stay or pack out in the rain. You should always make every effort to locate your camp out of the wind, keep some clothes and your sleeping bag dry, and prepare for colder conditions. To wait out a long rain means you have to have sufficient food for that purpose. Having sufficient clothing for the later, colder weather, and the possible snow, is also a matter of preparation. Plan accordingly. Get the best forecasts you can.

Because a cold front might follow snowy or rainy weather, and because a squall line might follow hot, humid weather, you should be able to prepare for the worst case scenario: hurricane force winds, possible lightning, driving rain and much colder air. This kind of weather could occur at night!

The author has noted that the midday temperatures on top of the mountains in New Hampshire have usually been very close to (within ten degrees of) what they were early in the morning at home before he left. You should be able to determine some similar relationship for the mountains near your home.

There are many aspects of weather that escape prediction by an amateur. For instance, you may expect clear weather without knowing that very cold arctic air will drive the night time temperature down quite far. On the other hand, understanding that clear weather (high pressure) often involves cold air, should lead you to prepare for the worst.

It is difficult to predict how long a period of good weather will last unless you have access to a weather map or an extended forecast. Even then, forecasters find inclement weather cropping up contrary to the extended forecast.

Sometimes, the weather *is* better in the mountains than in the valleys. There have been days when the weather was suitable for hiking on the northern end of our mountain range but not to the south. Of course, the opposite can be true.

If you are in the middle of precipitation, you will have little to guide your prediction other than the temperature, wind speed, and wind direction. Presuming that you want better weather, you should hope for a decreasing temperature, a change to northwest winds, and an increase in wind followed by a breakup of the cloud cover (and maybe a spectacular sunset). When some clearing occurs and the wind shifts into the west, but not the northwest, you might experience some inclement weather in the near future as additional low pressure cells pass through your area.

SOURCES OF WEATHER FORECASTS

The first source that you should look for is National Oceanic and Atmospheric Administration (NOAA) broadcasts in your area. NOAA makes these broadcasts continuously on radio frequencies 162.400, 162.475, and 162.550 megahertz FM from transmitters scattered around the country (each transmitter uses only one of the three frequencies). These transmitters have a range of from fifty to one hundred miles. You will need a special receiver, called a **weather radio**, to receive these broadcasts. There are overlapping reception areas along the East coast. Many major cities have such transmitters nearby. Along the coasts broadcasts include marine forecasts. Forecasts are updated several times a day.

Flash flood, tornado, and storm warnings are repeated often when relevant. Some areas have forecasts for the mountains every fifteen minutes in the morning. Sometimes, the long range forecast is inserted only after several short-term forecast sequences. You may have to listen for longer than you would like to get to the forecast of interest.

It is possible to carry a battery powered weather radio with you into the mountains. However, see the discussion of ELECTRONIC AIDS in Chapter 13 in which I suggest that you should consider what kind of wilderness experience it is that you seek.

Another continuous broadcast of weather information is available on the Weather Channel. This is programming carried by most cable television services. While it will provide a picture of what is happening on a national scale, on a regional scale and locally, you may find little information about conditions specific for higher elevations in your mountains. You may have to wait through a great number of ads. I do like the Weather Channel forecasts, because they provide me with an understanding of the likely progression of events. The picture showing the radar detection of precipitation gives me a good idea about what to expect in the ensuing few hours. The storm system analyses, with projected positions, give me a reasonable idea as to what the next couple of days are likely to provide.

Many local radio stations carry regional weather forecasts that include forecasts for higher elevations. These may be available at only one time in the morning.

Your local airport may have a forecasting service you can access, probably at a price. Sometimes these meteorologists can customize the forecast when you provide the altitude and location of interest.

You might be able to find an Internet site that provides current weather conditions and/or forecasts for the mountain range of interest to you.

The weather is a critical element in the experience of anyone who spends his or her time outdoors. Weather is a deadly serious issue when at its worst. Get appropriate forecasts. Choose your weather. Make appropriate decisions as conditions change. Be prepared for the worst; carry the appropriate gear, and be prepared to turn back. ❋

7

NAVIGATION: A SENSE OF DIRECTION AND PLACE

If all you have ever needed to know were the two directions from uptown to downtown and back, you have new skills to learn! If you have never bushwhacked, you might never have had to develop a good sense of direction. Once you develop this sense, you may be uneasy when the trail (or road) you are traveling departs from the direction you expect it to take. That is the level of skill and awareness you want in order to stay on the right trail and to bushwhack to the desired destination. What is most necessary is remaining alert to what is around you. Notice how those surroundings relate to where you have been and are going.

To navigate is to determine where you are and the distance and direction to where you want to go. If you have a map, you can even pick the most favorable route and its sequence of legs with distinct distances and directions. This assumes that you can read a map. Some youngsters have a map concept by age five, and some adults never acquire this knowledge. I know a two and a half year old who recognizes a map when he sees one, and can identify water on the map. If you have trouble reading maps, *that* is the place to start. Practice, practice, practice. Use the legend. Study the contours. Understand the meaning of scale. Measure distances. Find your way from one place to another. Visualize the countryside. Tell yourself that if kids can do it, so can you.

Start with a road map of your state. Find where you live. Think of a friend who lives at least thirty miles away, and find on the map where your friend lives. Select at least four round about ways to get from your place to your friend's place. Now, find out how long each trip is. Locate any water you would cross. Your map may also show railroads. Will you cross any? Are there any mountains shown on the map? Can you visualize these? Are there any lakes along the routes? Can you visualize these? Are there any cities along the routes? Can you visualize the through roads in these cities? When you feel comfortable with this type of map, then move on to topographic maps, which have contours, and do the same visualization. Look for trails, streams, ridges, cols, steep slopes, trail junctions, north slopes, roads, buildings, power lines, mines, railroads, trailheads and shelters.

Some of you will need limited goals. I suggest that everyone who goes to the mountains, woods, or deserts needs to be able to:

1) Read a map,
2) Orient a map,
3) Take a compass bearing from a map and follow it, and
4) Take a compass bearing to a distant point, and lay that out on the map.

You do not have to learn map and compass skills alone. Hiking organizations do offer workshops. Another opportunity may be available to you as orienteering events. Try the latter with a friend who knows the ropes.

A GPS unit will not help you unless you know the location (latitude and longitude) of your destination, something you probably will not be able to determine from the map. Even with latitude and longitude designation at every fifteen minutes of angle on the map, you are still lacking a means of interpolation. Worse, the GPS may be using a different **datum**[1] than the map. Many maps do not specify the datum. Early maps could be "off by a mile" both literally and figuratively.

---

[1] A geographical datum is the starting point and scheme for determining all latitudes and longitudes. My U.S.G.S. topographical maps for New Hampshire are based on the North American Datum of 1927. The datum accepted as the more universal is the North American Datum of 1983. In the Northeast latitudes and longitudes determined by the latter datum differ from those based on the former in being about four meters south and 38 meters west. If you read the instructions for a GPS unit, you should be able to reprogram the datum it uses. Do not forget to reprogram when you switch maps.

For those who wish to go beyond the simple concepts introduced here, or for those who need to see the same material presented in a different way, I recommend that you read *The Essential Wilderness Navigator* by Seidman or *Be Expert With Map And Compass* (or later books) by Kjellstrom.

In this chapter I will leave out as many complications as is prudent. I have used several simplifications to which the experts might take exception. The point is to try to keep it simple.

A SENSE OF DIRECTION AND PLACE

If someone left you in the middle of the woods on a sunny day, could you tell north from south? Could you walk to the west all day as the sun's position changed? Could you walk 100 paces north, east, south and then west so as to reach the starting point?

In order to have a sense of direction, it helps to know in which directions north and south are. If the sun is out, you will see it in the south at noontime. This assumes that you are in the northern temperate zone (most of the U.S. and Canada). There is a small variation throughout the year due to the nature of the earth's orbit. There is daylight saving's time to consider. And there is a dependence upon your east-west location within the time zone. For your location, determine the compass direction of the sun at 12:00 noon for the time of year when you will be hiking. You should also determine the direction of the sun relative to true north, a manipulation I will discuss later.

In the morning the sun is farther east than it will be at noon. You can get a sense of where the sun will be at noon, if you know how long it will be until noon. The sun will be almost east (true) at 6:00 a.m., and almost west at 6:00 p.m. At other times in the morning you can obtain your concept of south by judging how far the sun must have gone from east toward south. The opposite direction from south is north. Many people working in the woods or bushwhacking all day long need only the sun to keep themselves oriented. Note that you can measure the directions discussed here to within about ten or fifteen degrees. Celestial navigation (the kind that offshore sailors use) can be much more precise. When you know the direction of north and south by using your compass, you can determine the approximate time by observing the direction of the sun.

Photo 4-1 Bottom Ice
This is also known as "anchor ice." It forms when the air temperature remains below freezing for an extended period. If it stays cold long enough, the brook will freeze over with a small residual flow, either at the bottom, or on the top.

Photo 4-2 Whiteout
Notice that there are footprints in the foreground, but those in the background are hard to find.

Photo 6-1   Thunderstorm Cloud
This picture shows a fully developed thunderstorm cloud, which has ice crystals (the non-turbulent upper part) at higher altitiude. The ice crystals spread at the top to form an anvil shaped cloud.
Photo graciously provided by George Howe.

Photo 6-2   An Inversion Layer
The grayish, low haze is smoke trapped in an inversion layer. The picture was taken from Mt. Moriah (NH) looking toward Great Gulf.
Mt. Washington is to the left.

Photo 6-3   Fair Weather Cumulus Clouds
The lower, puffy clouds are fair weather cumulus clouds, which may increase in sky coverage as the day progresses. The upper clouds may be part of an approaching warm front and bear watching. The schooners are a frequent sight on the Maine coast between Rockland and Bar Harbor.

Photo 6-4   Cirrus Clouds
These wispy clouds often appear as mare's tails or as a mackeral sky. They can be the first phase of a sequence we call a warm front.

Photo 6-5   Cirrostratus Clouds
The thin hazy clouds in the foreground are cirrostratus complicated by a jet trail (contrail). The clouds in the background appear to be altostratus. The bright spot just over the ridge is a sun dog caused by sunlight reflected from horizontal ice crystals in the air (wind blown in this case).

Photo 6-6   Altostratus Clouds

Photo 6-7 Stratus Clouds
These stratus clouds over Mt. Washington (NH) have been modified by orographic winds. Rain is likely in the near future. The picture was taken from Monroe Flats. Notice the profusion of sandwort in bloom.

**Photo 8-1
Trail Corridor**

Photo 8-2   The Appalachian Trail in Winter
The trail goes just to the right of center, and then diagonally to the left.
This picture was taken in Vermont in a year with much snow.

**Photo 9-1
A Campsite in
the Bugaboos**
This campsite is some-
what protected from
avalanches and rockfall.

**Photo 9-2
Snow Trench**
A trench was cut, covered with dead branches and then covered with snow.

Photo 10-1   Glissades
Two climbers are descending late in the day from Symmetry Spire in the Grand Tetons by means of a standing and a squatting glissade. They are prepared to execute self-arrests.

Photo 10-2 Emergency Snowshoe
The construction is described in the text.

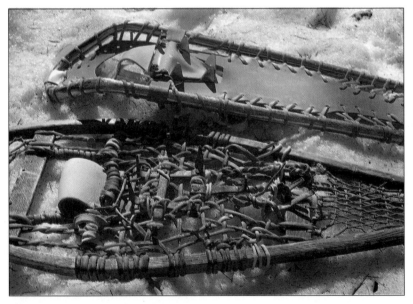

Photo 10-3 Snowshoe Creepers
In the foreground is a wooden snowshoe with half of an U.S. Army crampon attached. In the background is a Sherpa® snowshoe with a Tucker Claw® binding, which I recommend for mountain hiking. The inventer of this binding is Dick Tucker, who is shown in Photo 6-2.

If it is a cloudy day, and the clouds are moving right along, you can use the direction of their travel as a direction reference, provided the wind does not shift at cloud level. For a period of a few hours, clouds can serve. Wind near the ground is not as dependable. It is particularly fickle on the lee, or downwind, side of large hills. If the wind on the windward side of the hill is blowing from the west, on the leeward side one may find that it will blow first from the south (perpendicular to the flow on the windward side of the hill) and then from the north. Turbulence causes this changing of the direction of the wind.

You need a sense of direction and distance traveled to keep your sense of place relative to some starting point. When there are many changes in direction (with their corresponding distances), it is helpful to plot those sequentially on a map. We refer to this as a dead (slang for deduced) reckoning plot. This will provide you with an updated map location and assist you in maintaining a sense of place. It helps if you can identify the physical and cultural features in your vicinity that the map shows, such as mountains, rivers, valleys, lakes and all the features mentioned earlier. First, we need the skill to find direction with sufficient accuracy to make a meaningful plot.

COMPASS READING

If it is a cloudy day with no sun, or if it is dark and there are no stars, then you will want a compass in order to determine direction. To read a compass, remove from the vicinity of where you will work all steel objects and any other magnets (a compass is a magnet). If you are indoors, be careful to determine whether or not the wooden table you use has metal fastenings underneath. The red end of the compass needle points towards magnetic north.

A **compass bearing** is the horizontal direction from one place to another expressed as an angle measured clockwise from magnetic north. The angle specified designates a particular direction. See Figure 7-1, on the following page, which shows a compass as you would use it to measure the angle.

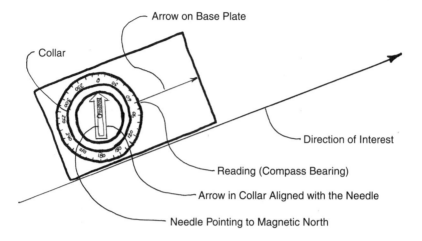

Figure 7-1: Using A Compass To Measure A Compass Bearing

Here's how to take a compass bearing (I will assume you have a Silva®
compass or a similar make):

1) Hold the compass level (horizontal) in front of you, or
   place the compass on a rock, stump or other object high
   enough so that you can line your eye up with the side of
   the horizontal, stationary compass.

2) Line up the side of the compass with the direction to
   some object of interest, such as a peak that you can
   identify. You want the arrow on the base plate of the
   compass to point *toward* the object of interest.

3) Without turning the base plate of the compass, turn the
   round collar so that the arrow in the center of the collar
   lines up with the red (north) end of the compass needle.
   Check to make sure that you still have the edge of the
   base plate lined up with the peak.

4) Now read the compass bearing by finding the mark on
   the collar that you aligned with the arrow on the base
   plate of the compass.

Since there are 360 degrees in a complete circle, there are 90 degrees in a
quarter circle, and there are five or ten degrees associated with each of the
longer markings around the collar. Most compasses have marks for each
degree or for each two degree. You should find a number at least every thirty
degrees. You only need to read the bearing to the nearest mark, but you may,
if you wish, estimate the amount in between marks (interpolate).

Did you worry about using the edge of the compass rather than the centerline? The two lines are parallel, and have the same direction for our purposes.

Compare what you are doing with Figure 7-1. Ask yourself if the result you obtained makes sense. Pick up the compass, turn the collar, place it down again, and repeat this alignment procedure as many times as it takes for you to assure yourself that you have a repeatable reading.

MAP READING

You need to be able to read a topographical map, because the map is the source of information about how to get from one place to another. The principal characteristics of a **topographical map** (one that shows the topography, usually by means of contours) are its scale and its contour interval. The **scale** refers to the ratio by which the size has been reduced from full size. If the map has a scale such that one inch represents one mile, then the **scale factor** is expressed as 1 : 63,360 or just 63,360 (There are 63,360 inches in a mile.). If the scale factor is large, the dictionary says that we have a **small-scale** map. Distances look small on a small-scale map. Usage is not uniform; there is confusion between scale and scale factor. To be definitive you could say that you have a map with a **large scale factor** when the scale factor is large.

The **contour interval** refers to the vertical separation of the horizontal planes represented by the contour lines, or the vertical rise between two places shown on the map on their respective, adjacent contour lines. Most maps have a statement at the bottom something like "Contour Interval = 50 feet." If the map does not provide the contour interval, then you can infer it from the elevations marked on contour lines. However, this leaves in doubt whether the elevations are in feet, meters, or some other units.

A topographical map provides more than contours. Man-made features (cultural features) such as roads, houses, etc., are shown in black. Water is shown in blue. Topography (contour lines) is usually shown in green or brown. Sometimes there is green shading to distinguish the forested portions.

Figure 7-2, on the next page, shows a black and white representation of a segment of a contour map (Tuckerman's Ravine in New Hampshire).

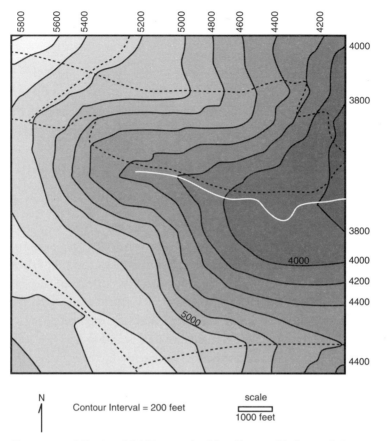

Figure 7-2: A Portion Of A Topographic Map Showing Tuckerman's Ravine

Figure 7-3 shows a computer generated 3-dimensional view (bird's eye perspective) of the same space as seen from the northeast. (Figure 7-4, on the following page, shows the same valley from the northwest, and Figure 7-5 shows it from the southwest.) The contours appear as if someone went out and painted horizontal lines at contour elevations over the countryside. No vertical exaggeration has been used.

Notice where the stream is. Notice how the valley, in which the stream flows, is shown by the topo lines having bends that have the concave side towards the downstream direction. Notice how the trail goes up the mountain. The contour interval is 200 feet. This means that there are 200 feet of elevation difference between the contour lines. It also means that the numbers on the contour lines are elevations in feet. On the map you can read how many topo lines the trail crosses, and find

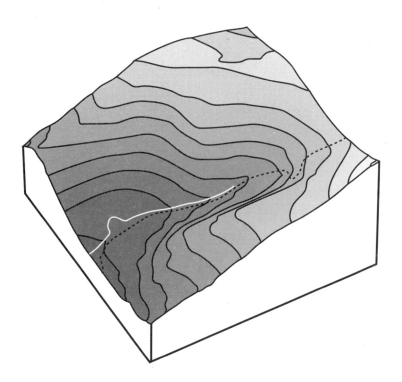

Figure 7-3: A Perspective View Of Tuckerman's Ravine From The Northeast

out how much elevation gain there is. It is important to understand that the contour lines in the valleys will appear concave towards the downhill, and the contour lines on ridges will appear convex toward the downhill direction. You really need to master this, because this is the way you tell ridges from valleys when there is no designation of a brook to help make the distinction. Start by determining which contours are lower and which are higher. Then look for ridges and valleys based on the concave, convex nature.

If you read the map of your favorite hiking area long enough and with sufficient care, you can visualize the shape of the mountains and valleys. If you carefully study the map of country you have never been in, you can visualize it too. I have found that this visualization, learning something about what is around every bend in the river, took some of the adventure out of a wilderness canoe trip. It made it safer, because we could anticipate the hazardous sections.

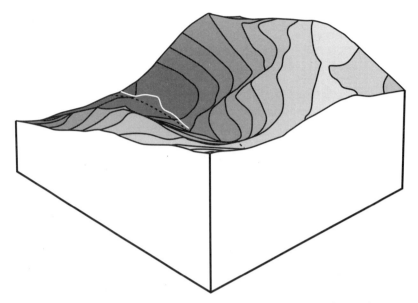

Figure 7-4: A Perspective View Of Tuckerman's Ravine From The Northwest

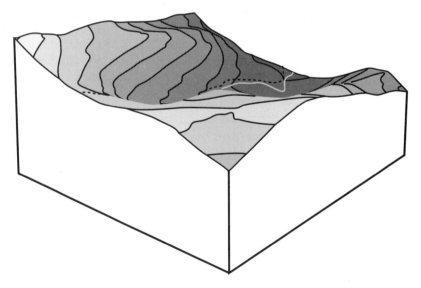

Figure 7-5: A Perspective View Of Tuckerman's Ravine From The Southwest

ORIENTING A MAP

You can accomplish the simplest navigation when working with an oriented map, since in that case all magnetic directions between points on the map are parallel to magnetic directions between the corresponding real locations. This provides the opportunity to work only with magnetic bearings, ignoring any reference to true north. It provides the easiest means to determining compass bearings to points of interest that you cannot see from where you are.

To orient a map, you turn it in a horizontal plane until the magnetic north arrow on the map lines up with magnetic north. This is a direction determined by use of a compass. Step by step instructions are given below. The true north arrow on any map will line up with true north when you have oriented the map. The magnetic north arrow on the map will line up with magnetic north when you have oriented the map.

U.S.G.S. topographic maps and most trail maps have a pair of arrows that join, usually on the upper left border. One arrow points straight up towards the top of the map, and indicates true north. It might be labeled with a "T" or "N." The other arrow points on the map towards magnetic north and is labeled with an "M" or "MN." We call the angle between these arrows **magnetic declination**. See Figure 7-6 in which the declination, the angle between the arrows, is specified as 15 degrees and the declination is to the west.

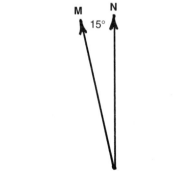

Figure 7-6 — Arrows Found On Most Maps

However, some strip maps of trails do not have north at the top. And some of these show only the direction to true north. Most maps based on the Universal Transverse Mercator grid system will not have true north at the top. It is important for you to look for the direction of magnetic north on the map you are using.

If the map does not have these little arrows, you need to know how much and which way the declination is in order to draw your own arrows and to properly orient a map. You should assume that the vertical direction towards the top of the map represents true north. You should find the declination specified somewhere on the map. A declination to the west means that the magnetic arrow would be to the left of the true north arrow. In this case you subtract declination from the magnetic bearing to obtain the true bearing (measured from true north). A declination to the east means that you add declination to the magnetic bearing to obtain a true bearing. If we had not worked with an oriented map and had made reference to vertical lines on the map pointing to true North, the conversion from true bearings to magnetic bearings would involve adding or subtracting magnetic declination. The addition or subtraction is not difficult, but remembering when to add or subtract stumps many people.

Fortunately, most maps do have magnetic north arrows. You can orient these maps just by lining the compass needle up with the magnetic north arrow on the map and without having to do any figuring. It is easiest, if you:

1) Line up the zero degree mark on the collar with the arrow on the base plate of the compass,

2) Align the edge of the compass base plate with the magnetic north arrow on the map, and

3) Turn the map and compass in a *horizontal* plane until the red (north) end of the compass needle lines up with the arrow inside the collar.

Once you have oriented the map, the line between two mountains shown on the map is parallel to the line between the corresponding real mountains. Both lines will have the same magnetic direction or compass bearing. This is essentially true whether you are in the woods or at home when you orient the map. If your home is within two hundred miles of the mountains, the error (difference in declination) is likely to be no more than a couple of degrees. The oriented map is the most useful, because it shows the proper directions from a location of interest on the map to other features on the same map.

TAKING COMPASS BEARINGS TO AND FROM A MAP

BEARINGS TAKEN TO THE MAP FROM THE FIELD: If you do not know exactly where you are but you can identify a peak, then you can take a compass bearing toward that peak, as described earlier. What you find is the direction from you to the peak, not the direction from the peak to you. You can plot that line on your map. To do so, it is easiest if you orient the map first. Spread it out on a horizontal surface (right side up!) so that the magnetic north arrow is towards magnetic north (Set your compass on zero, line it up with magnetic north arrow and rotate the map). Then take the bearing to the peak with the compass on a rock or post. Place the compass on the map, and align one edge of the compass base plate with the peak. Then rotate the base plate around the peak until the red end of the compass needle lines up with the arrow attached to the collar. The edge of the compass passing over the peak is now on a line that runs from you to the peak. You can draw that line on the map.

Remember that the arrow on the base of the compass points from you to the peak, so the direction from the peak to you is the opposite. We refer to this as a **back bearing**. If the compass reading toward the peak is 180 degrees or more, subtract 180 degrees to obtain the back bearing. If the compass bearing to the peak is less than 180 degrees, add 180 degrees to obtain the back bearing.

If you are on a trail, ridge or stream that you can identify on the map, then note where the line you have drawn intersects the representation of the trail, ridge or stream. You are at the location (intersection) you have found (within the errors of the method).

If you are not on a linear feature, such as a trail, ridge or stream, you still can find your location on the map. You now need two peaks you can identify. To use this method (called **triangulation**), just repeat what you did above for one or two more peaks. The two (or more) lines on the map cross at your location (within the limitations of the method). This method works best, if you:

1) Choose peaks in directions from you separated by about 90 degrees,
2) Can place the compass on a stationary object like a rock or stump, and
3) Measure bearings carefully.

BEARINGS TAKEN TO THE FIELD FROM THE MAP: Sometimes you want to determine if a peak you see is the one you think it is on the map. To do this, you can orient the map and sight along the map, or you can take a bearing from the map. To do the latter, orient the map and lay the edge of your compass base along the line from the place on the map that represents where you are to the peak on the map. The arrow on the base plate must face towards the peak. Rotate the collar until the arrow inside the collar lines up with the red end of the compass needle. Then you can read the bearing from the compass. Set the compass on a rock, and sight along the edge to find out if the peak you see is in the right direction. If you have the right peak, the compass needle will line up with the arrow in the collar.

Some people find it convenient to draw on their map a series of lines about an inch apart parallel to the magnetic north arrow, so-called "**magnetic north lines.**" You can use these in taking bearings to and from the map without having to orient the map, and you never have to become involved with magnetic declination. The technique involves placing the base of the compass along the line between two points of interest on the map, and turning the collar until the arrow attached to it lines up with the magnetic north lines. Ignore the compass needle. You can read the magnetic compass direction of the line of interest indicated on the compass. Be careful to take the bearing from you to the object of interest, and not the opposite direction. Also, be careful that the arrow inside the compass collar is pointing towards magnetic north, not south. The reason I did not introduce magnetic north lines earlier is that you may be called on to use someone's map that does not have the lines.

TRAVELING BY COMPASS BEARING: Now, suppose you want to go to a peak that you cannot see, because of the trees or hills in the way. If you take a bearing from the map as described in the last paragraph, this would give you the direction to follow to reach your objective. In practice, you cannot go straight through the woods. You have to offset to get around each tree, boulder or knob in your way. Keep track of the offsets, and try to go first one way and then the other. If you can see a feature some distance ahead in the direction in which you want to go, then go to that feature by the easiest way.

Regardless of how good the visibility is, it is wise to monitor the compass direction in which you are traveling. Do this in order to confirm that you are on the correct trail and to give you the direction to use when going back down the trail (back bearing).

Summer or winter, in advance of your trip, it is helpful to plot lines (with bearings) on your map along the directions you wish to go, particularly for long traverses above tree line. This is particularly helpful in a whiteout, in thick fog, and when unexpected snowfall obliterates the trail. Recording on your map the magnetic compass bearing of the trail makes it possible to quickly check that direction, if you become disoriented in a howling gale. On one traverse of a mountain I needed only one compass bearing to get down off the summit. I worked it out in advance, and set the compass before the trip (remembering the bearing so I could check that the compass had not shifted). When I reached the summit I pulled the compass out briefly in the howling snowstorm. Try it; you will impress your friends. Someday it might save your life.

Establishing bearings from a map in a windy rainstorm is difficult, and you are likely to lose or destroy the map. If you do the navigation in advance, you can keep the map in a plastic bag while you read the compass bearing that you previously wrote on the map. Navigating with pre-plotted bearings in comfortable circumstances is good practice for bad conditions, as you are likely to do it rationally.

NAVIGATING ON THE MOUNTAIN

I offer the following exercise as practice in using the map and compass in a way that must become second nature to you. Try it on a day with good visibility. It is not a good idea to start learning navigation when the weather is bad or when you need the information to survive.

Now, let's use the map in the field, starting at a trailhead. This is a place that is easy to find on your trail map, because the intersection of a road and the trail defines it. For this instruction, it would be helpful, if you could actually read this at the trailhead, and if you could use a small scale factor map, such as those used in orienteering.

When you start hiking up the trail, note on a clipboard the time when you start and the direction of travel determined from your compass by taking the compass bearing of the trail:

   1) Point the arrow on the base plate of the compass down
       the trail (in the direction you plan to go),

2) Turn the collar until the arrow inside lines up with the
   compass needle, and

3) Read the bearing.

The first part of the hike probably will not be very steep, and you will be able to hike at an average rate of about two miles per hour. Note the direction you travel. You probably will have to mentally average the direction as you progress. Every fifteen minutes, stop and assess where you are on the map both by estimating the direction and distance you have traveled, and by comparing what you see around you with what the map shows. If there is a lot of area crammed into the map (large scale factor), then you will have to travel farther to see the changes along the trail as represented on the map. This is also true if the map shows poorly differentiated terrain (few distinguishing features). If you continue this process of checking your estimate of how far you have traveled with what the map shows, and comparing that to your surroundings, you should be able to keep track of where you are. You can then keep your sense of place. If you practice all of the techniques of navigating, you will gain confidence.

When hiking, pay attention to your surroundings, from those at your feet to those on the horizon. Note when the trail is on a ridge. Watch for the point at which it leaves the ridge, since this is a feature you should be able to find on your map. All major stream crossings provide you with locations you can find on the map. All trail junctions are important landmarks. Every significant col or saddle gives you a reference point. Remember, in order to know where you are, you need to keep track of these landmarks by following your progress on the map. You can estimate where you are in between landmarks based on the time you have been hiking since you passed the last significant feature shown on the map. To do this you need to know your average rate of travel from previous experience.

You can determine how high you are by using your **line of sight** (the line from you to the distant point toward which you are looking) to the distant horizon. That line of sight to the horizon will intersect nearby hills at your elevation. As an example, if you are high enough so that you can see the summit of a nearby mountain even with or in line with the distant horizon, then your elevation will be approximately that of the nearby summit. Find the elevation of the nearby summit from your map. Then locate where your trail reaches the same elevation. That will be your approximate location.

When weather conditions make it difficult to see distant landmarks, useful indicators of your approximate location include observation of changes in the vegetation as the elevation changes, geologic or topographic character of the terrain, compass direction of the trail, steepness of the trail, distance to a nearby brook, and the quantity of water in the brook (it should decrease as you approach the upper end). Here is where the pre-plotted compass bearings of the trail would be helpful.

Even on a clear day on a mountain top, clouds sometimes envelop you on short notice, greatly reducing visibility and adding to confusion and discomfort. So, you should be using all the clues you can find to identify where you are before and after the clouds arrive.

WHAT TO DO WHEN YOU ARE LOST

You could experience the emotion of being lost whenever you lose visibility and your sense of place. You might also feel lost when you find yourself without a map in country you do not recognize. The experience is more likely to occur when you are not on a well-defined trail.

In a wilderness that you do not know, losing track of your landmarks results in uncertainty about where you are and your sense of place becomes more general. We also know that as being "somewhat lost." Even though you cannot identify the landmarks, you should know what part of the state you are in and which direction the major rivers and highways go. Often, in wilderness travel the streams and watershed divides define the country for you. Eventually, you recover from this condition of being somewhat lost when you reach recognizable landmarks. So, being lost can be a cause for panic or it can be seen as a rather relative matter. You cannot change the nature of the difficult travel needed to reach the road, but you can adjust your outlook about the threat to you of being lost. Certainly, the more experience you have bushwhacking, the less threat you should perceive when somewhat lost. Always keep the bigger picture in mind.

Surely, you have heard that you are supposed to stay calm when you find that you are lost. It does take discipline, particularly when you are under assault by zillions of black flies (or mosquitos) and the sun is setting. If there is any preparation you might make for this condition it is to buy bug dope, start early, and hone your navigation skills. Orienteering is an excellent way to develop and practice those skills.

When somewhat lost you know something about the general location you are in, and you also know roughly how long and in which direction you have traveled since you last knew your location. So, start by consulting your map and trying to plot your approximate location.

Next, identify the watershed. In which direction does the nearest stream flow? Can you identify a valley you are in, and what is the downstream compass direction? Do you see anything like it on the map? Can you see any roads; does your map show them? What can you hear? Is there anything in the general direction from which you have come that you can identify? Could you gain more perspective by climbing to a ridge? Have you come through or past a particular vegetative type or geological formation that you can identify from that ridge? Are there peaks around which you did not identify before, but which you recognize. If you remain calm, you can think clearly through the logical process. Keep up the blood sugar by eating enough to compensate for the calories you have burned throughout the day.

It helps to play this game before you go a long way from country you can identify. Think like an early explorer. Keep track of where you are going, so that you will have the means to return. If you are uncertain as to whether you are going in the right direction or whether you are on the trail, it is wiser to go back to your last known point than to forge on ahead.

Lacking any other information, the standard advice for those who are lost is to follow a stream downhill. This is good advice, if your knowledge of the "known world" outside your local, unidentified world includes a road downstream. If you do not know what is downstream, you should seriously consider returning the way you came. The downstream route could involve impossible chasms or a hundred miles of bushwhacking.

When you become disoriented on a gray day, it is easy to wonder about the accuracy of your compass. Trust your compass as long as the needle swings freely when the compass is in a horizontal plane. Some people carry two compasses. When they both point in the same direction, it is very convincing. My brother and I discovered this after hunting in a thick softwoods we now call Allen's Folly, but that is another story.

Navigation is the art of keeping a sense of place and determining the direction and distance to a destination. It takes practice and staying tuned in to the conditions around you. Don't die on the mountain; navigate your way back. ❄

TRAIL FINDING

Practical mountain travel anywhere starts with a study of the latest edition of any published trail guides which might include trail maps and descriptions. Other useful maps include the 7.5 minute series of topographical maps published by the U.S. Geological Survey.

You may find it difficult to find trailheads. The U.S. Forest Service, the National Park Service, and other groups responsible for trail maintenance erect trail signs at the trailheads. However, some signs are located a short distance along the trail away from the road to reduce vandalism. Trailheads outside the forests and parks are not so well marked. The hiker should refer to the trail guide for directions to particular trailheads. The guidebook may indicate how a particular trail is marked or found. If the trailhead is obscure, I suggest that you start at a well-known trailhead and finish at the more obscure end. If you spot a car near the obscure trailhead, place it near distinctive landscape features, so you will know which way to go on the road when you finish your hike.

If the trail crosses a farm or logging operation, it may be necessary to search the far side or inquire locally.

The thick brush on some of the Appalachian mountains and the coast ranges of the West Coast does not allow the easy cross-country travel found on some of the Rocky Mountains and elsewhere at high altitude. When hiking on wooded mountains, you should use the available trails until you have mastered woods navigation. Even on trails, nature reduces the information about the trail by means of blown down trees, leaves in the trail, and wind-toppled cairns. She also confuses trail finders with her own corridors and the natural pruning of trees along the weather side of ridges. Seldom-used or poorly maintained trails are often difficult to follow. If the trail you are on has not been maintained, sometimes you must choose a possible route based on experience as to how the trail is likely to go and how it might look. To follow difficult trails requires identification of subtle clues along the way and staying alert.

When the person in the front of the hiking party comes to a place where he or she cannot see where the trail goes, often the next person in line may spot a clue that the first person could not see. It pays to have two or more people on the lookout for the trail. Sometimes, everyone has to search.

When you go above tree line, be very careful to note how the trail looks behind you. When you return and descend toward the tree line, the trail opening is often obscure. For hiking purposes, I consider the **tree line** (also referred to as the timberline) to be the interface between where trees grow greater than head height and where they are shorter. The forester and the botanist may have other definitions. Above tree line you may be following a line of **cairns** (man-made piles of stone, usually cone shaped). Even with good visibility, trail junctions and signs may be confusing without careful study of the map and the trail descriptions in your trail guidebook.

The trail **treadway** (the worn path underfoot) may be easy or difficult to follow depending on the amount of use made of the trail and whether the trail is on grass, sand, woods duff, stones or glacier. A lightly used trail through a field with no man-made features, and a trail through open hardwoods with leaves covering the treadway (with corridors in all directions), can be very hard to follow. In these circumstances, and in many winter conditions, the hiker relies heavily on blazes and cairns.

When you feel uncertain that you are on the trail, or when you can find no further corridor or treadway, go back to the last place where you were certain that you were on the trail (usually a blaze). Considering my experience, you will save time by going back rather than wandering around ahead. After going back, begin your search going slowly and checking all possibilities. On poorly maintained trails the challenge is great. After exhausting all possibilities, then you can begin to cast about ahead and to the sides. Do not forget the possibility of a switchback.

In finding a trail, sometimes the problem is that of making sure you are on the correct trail. When you come to an intersection, it is important to ask yourself in which compass direction the trail goes that you want and whether it ascends or descends from that point. The trail signs might be missing, or someone might have maliciously turned them.

When you look at the map, does the trail stay on the west side of the brook? How many brook crossings are there? Are these crossings of the same brook or different brooks? You cannot cross the same brook from left bank to right bank twice in a row when facing the same flow direction unless it is an ephemeral stream, one that disappears underground occasionally. Are there any switchbacks? How many does the map show? Does the trail start out steep, or is it nearly level? Does the trail stay on the west side of the mountain, or does it wind around onto the north side? It helps to pay attention to all the clues on your map and in the field.

TRAIL FINDING IN WOODS

Trails in woods consist of treadways, corridors and man-made features, such as blazes and evidence of pruning. The trees or underbrush on either side of the trail and overhead define a corridor. See Photo 8-1

Your trail guidebook will usually tell you what color of painted blazes you will find on each trail. It helps to know that white blazes are used on the Appalachian Trail, except along the Gulfside Trail (in N.H.) where rocks painted yellow are found on top of cairns. White blazes are also used on other through trails, such as the Long Trail in Vermont, and on several Greenways in New Hampshire. On one section of the Appalachian Trail in a birch forest in Maine dark borders (or backgrounds) have been painted around the white blazes on white trees. The majority of side trails are blazed with blue paint. Other major trails may have red, yellow or orange blazes. Double blazes (one blaze over another) are used to indicate significant changes in direction of the trail or approach to a trail junction or stream crossing. According to the convention generally used in the East when the upper blaze is not directly over the lower blaze, this indicates that the trail changes direction toward the side to which the upper blaze is offset.

If you are having trouble finding the blazes, it is often helpful to look back down the trail for blazes in the opposite direction. They not only confirm that you are on the trail but they usually face the direction in which you should be traveling.

Old axe blazes, axe cuts on tree trunks at about chest height, can be confused with natural scars, but confusion is less likely when blazes appear on opposite sides of a tree or lie along some line of march. At sharp bends in a trail, the blazes may be on sides of the tree at right angles. On some trails these axe blazes were painted, and the remains of that paint might be present. Note that boundary surveyors also use axe blazes, painted and unpainted, along property boundaries. The edges of land acquired to protect the Appalachian Trail have round, yellow blazes. The borders of State lands in New Hampshire have round or oval blue blazes. The boundaries of some federal lands (National Parks and National Forests) have red blazes. Each timber company will have its own color. If you are on a trail that is marked with the customary 2 inch by 6 inch rectangular blazes, oval blazes for a boundary, even of the same color, should be distinguishable.

Occasionally you will find large areas of trees blown over by high winds (**blow downs**). These are very difficult to cross. It helps to identify the corridor on the far side, if possible. You have two choices: follow the treadway through the blow down carefully, or follow the boundary of the blow down.

Sometimes the only clue to a trail is the stubs of branches showing where someone pruned to clear it. Note that maintainers will generally prune only one side of a tree. Another clue consists of the sawn ends of logs that were cut to clear the trail. In climates where lichens grow on rocks, wear will show on the larger rocks in the treadway. Trails used by winter hikers may acquire scratches on the rocks, made by crampons.

Trails often lie along natural terrain features, such as exposed bedrock and natural openings along ridges. You can also find the trail in the lee of ledges on more exposed stretches. Sometimes you find the trail following openings created by mud slides or snow avalanches. These scars may be hazardous routes during heavy rains or when snow covered. If you must climb a slide scar, the safer route, though more difficult, is along the edge of the slide.

Occasionally, one must go to the very end of a long corridor to see where the next stretch of corridor goes. At times, when no corridor is evident, you may only be able to find the trail by imagining where it might go if it was not for the fallen tree, the fallen limb, the snowdrift, or other material in your foreground.

A trail may follow for a distance what was a road. If the trail has been poorly maintained, you will have to remain quite alert in order to recognize the place where the trail leaves the road.

In the summer, one could lose sight of the trail ahead and behind, and not know in which direction to go. This a good reason to stay alert and to keep track of the direction of the trail.

Summits are places where hikers who are not navigating can become confused. It is not uncommon for them to go down the wrong trail, particularly when the trails are poorly differentiated. Be careful to keep your sense of direction. It is a good habit to look back at the trail you have come up as you approach a summit. This will help you recognize the correct trail when you are ready to descend. It will be particularly helpful if the visibility deteriorates.

TRAIL FINDING IN WINTER WOODS

Trail finding in winter is much more difficult than finding the same trail in summer. Less information about the trail is available when snow has covered it. However, the hollow of a worn treadway might show through two or three feet of snow, if the snow has not been wind blown. If the wind has blown the snow, there may be many hollows across the trail. In open hardwoods the vistas are similar in all directions. At best, the undergrowth appearing through the snow will be a little more noticeable on either side of the trail. If deep snow has covered the blazes, the trail in open woods is lost to the person who does not know it well.

The typical unbroken winter trail in woods consists of a corridor with a smooth, unbroken white carpet that has a width defined by trees and underbrush. See Photo 8-1 again, but now notice the carpet. Occasionally, the carpet may have trees (with no branches) in the middle of it, but this is less common than the unbroken carpet. To follow this carpet, you look ahead attempting to see where the next section of corridor goes after the bend of the stretch you are hiking. Try to look through the trees to see the next stretch. Seeing it means that you probably are still on the trail. Remember that the next stretch of trail might be around a switchback. When you come to a point where there are two or more corridors (and carpets) leading away from your present corridor, the one that goes straight ahead is the more likely continuation of the trail.

In the smaller softwoods and mixed growth, the primary clues are the corridors and stubs of branches where the trail maintainers have pruned the trees. In large softwoods with no understory (brush and shorter trees growing under the taller trees), one faces the same problem as in open hardwoods.

Photo 8-2 shows the Appalachian Trail in Vermont where it crosses open hardwoods. In the Photo there are apparent corridors going both to the left and to the right. After studying the scene for a number of minutes I discovered a faint blaze on a tree in the center foreground. It is too faint to show in the Photo. The Trail goes just right of center and then turns diagonally to the left. The snow was deep and covered whatever limbs and bushes might have otherwise indicated a corridor.

Often the hiker finds a corridor (or carpet) termination with no apparent trail leading away from that point. Sometimes this occurs when a downed tree blocks the trail at the eye level of the winter hiker, though it may be quite open to the summer hiker. In this case you may see the carpet continuing, though a tree blocks the corridor above the carpet. In such cases the hiker can find the trail at some short distance beyond, continuing in the same direction as before. Sometimes you have to imagine what a possible carpet would look like if it were not for bent over bushes. Tree limbs can fall with their butts down and look like bushes. Keep your mind open to all sorts of possibilities, and observe carefully.

You will know that you have lost the corridor when the trail breaking becomes substantially more difficult, the brush coming through the snow looks as though it should not be there, there seem to be a lot of blow downs, or there are young trees discernible just below the carpet.

Below tree line in the winter you are not lost; usually the snowshoe track behind you can lead you back. However, in a snowstorm the high winds can obliterate that track back to your car. That is a good reason to keep track of the compass direction in which you are traveling. On a sunny day use the direction of the sun and the time as a reference.

When you reach tree line in the winter, the ground may be ice covered, and your crampons or snowshoes may leave no track to follow back. Even if the ground is snow covered, your tracks may blow away before you return, as we experienced on Mt. Katahdin's Tableland. We were glad we had put in wands even though the weather was clear as we ascended (I described wands in Chapter 4 under "Whiteout"). Above tree line you might be following ice axe shaft holes that do not fill in with blowing snow as fast as you might expect. These holes show up better than crampon tracks, and you can make them deliberately in fairly hard crust which the crampons fail to mark. However, if it is snowing hard, you may want to plant wands or something similar. In the past people used softwood branches, but it is now illegal to cut them in most parks.

When following the snowshoe track of some previous party, it is important to remain alert to the possibility that, either the previous party was not going where you intend to go, or the previous party lost the trail, and ultimately went somewhere else. Timber and boundary surveyors, and hunters, may use a trail intermittently, leaving it when they come close to a destination of importance to them. Likewise, it is easy to follow an animal track off the trail into open woods. The larger animals like to follow trails as the easiest routes through the woods, but they will often leave a trail where it changes direction.

Winter hikers must know their trailheads well, since snow often buries signs and clues.

Above tree line in winter ice sufficiently thick to make the signs unreadable may cover everything. Removing the ice would destroy the signs, unless it is rime ice ("frost feathers"), which you can easily brush off the surface. Finding the compass direction of the trail you wish to take from that junction is something you could do in advance.

In the Northeast in a normal winter, the snow depth between 3500 feet in elevation and tree line will usually become as much as four feet or more. With that much snow the carpet may be only two or three feet below the overhead branches (the canopy). Still, the carpet may be apparent. Late in winter along some stretches, snow may fill the trail up to the canopy of branches. This condition occurs most commonly near tree line where drifting snow may accumulate. Since no information is available to the hiker, the trail, in effect, no longer exists. Walking among the tree tops along the trail may be no more or less difficult than walking among the trees off the trail. You may be able to proceed by using natural openings and terrain features leading in the same direction as the trail. Compass bearings and visual objectives may also be useful.

In the Northeast, late in the winter, along ridges from around 3000 feet to 5000 feet in elevation, the young softwood trees on either side of the trail become weighted with snow and ice. They bend into the trail effectively blocking it. At times you may be able to count on the trail going in a direction that is very difficult to pursue. A very dense growth of young, closely spaced softwoods may line the sides of the trail. It is maddening.

It is helpful to note that spruce traps (see Chapter 4) do not occur on the trail. If you find a spruce trap in the middle of your corridor, you may be only a couple of feet off the treadway, or you may be in a false corridor altogether.

Sometimes the trail follows an old road or railroad bed. The roadbed bed might not be obvious, but the species of trees growing there might be different from those on either side.

You might be following the faint hollow in the snow indicating the track made by other hikers or skiers before the last storm. Sometimes this track is apparent only to the feet when the snow packs differently on and off the old track.

You should not assume that you will always be able to follow a trail from blaze to blaze or cairn to cairn. Standards of blazing vary, and some difficult trails may only have a good blaze every tenth of a mile on average. In such cases you may be happy to find a scrap of paint remaining where a blaze once existed. Sometimes snow from a recent storm has plastered over the blazes you face. You may be able to follow the trail by looking for the blazes that face the opposite direction. The cairns or other trail markers may only occur at important changes in the nature of the trail, or snow may have buried them. They may be too far apart when the visibility is low. Keep your eyes open. Rely on the carpet more than any other feature.

If you want to learn the techniques of trail finding, be the first one in the group so you can continuously seek out the route.

TRAIL FINDING IN OPEN COUNTRY

On a clear day, hiking in open country is relatively easy, since you can see major landmarks and hills that define your location. Because of this advantage, trails often have no signs or blazes. To find your way you must keep track of where you are in terms of the ridges and valleys you encounter. The most significant feature defining the terrain is the separation of watersheds, major and minor, by ridges. So, you need a map that, at least, shows the drainages or watersheds. Then you will be able to go up the correct stream valley to reach the appropriate point on the next watershed. With this kind of navigation it is not so important to have a trail. Actually, you want to be defensive or cautious about using trails, since they might not go where you want to go. As with navigation in thick country, you need to keep track of where you are.

Most often, trails continue straight ahead unless there is a good reason to make a turn, such as a rock outcrop, a wet spot, or other obstruction. In treeless fields or valleys the trail may be obscure, and the practical approach often is to proceed by the easiest way to the end of the field or valley. One then looks for the trail leaving the field or valley. A compass bearing might be helpful, if the ground undulates, if the end of the valley is poorly defined, or if the visibility is poor. In the Rockies and Sierras tall sticks or fence posts set up at intervals may mark the trail through a treeless valley.

Trails do become very important when obstacles cover the ground, such as large boulders, sink holes, thick brush in washes, etc. Under these circumstances you will save considerable time and aggravation by making the effort to keep to the trail.

On rainy or snowy days, and in sandstorms, "eyeball" navigation may be impossible. If you risk traveling under such conditions, then you will want to keep track of direction and distance traveled, which you should plot on your map. In order to know the distance traveled, you should perfect your knowledge of how fast you walk on various kinds of terrain. The company you keep or strong winds might alter your normal pace. You can determine your speed by keeping track of the time it takes to go a known distance when the weather is good, and by noting how the adverse conditions affect your travel over stretches of the trail you can identify.

Note that there is a one way type of navigation that can beguile the unwary. When climbing a mountain on which the sides are poorly differentiated, such as some of the cone-shaped, snow-covered volcanic peaks in the West, uphill is well defined, and leads to the summit. All uphill directions converge. By contrast, all downhill directions diverge, and you need some other basis for finding the way. You should have a descent plan before you start up the mountain. Wands? Compass bearing? Probably both. If the visibility decreases, you will need every clue you can find.

Trail finding is the art of following a path no matter how obscure. It takes practice and staying tuned in to conditions around you. Trail finding and navigation should go hand in hand. Don't die on the mountain; find the trail back. ❋

CAMPING

We do not usually think of camping skills as bearing on survival. However, there are a number of camping situations in which one could make a fatal mistake. It is essential to locate the tent in a spot free from hazards. Working safely with gasoline is very important. Using tools safely is important. When you are several days walk from the trailhead and access to medical help, all of the hazards associated with the mundane operations of camping take on much significance.

LOCATING A CAMPSITE

Safety should be the first consideration in locating a campsite. You should not place your tent under dead trees or tree limbs. Avalanche tracks are not appropriate places to camp. Avoid rockfall from steep slopes. Trails that animals use at night are not suitable tent sites. Lightning is an important consideration.

To avoid lightning look for sharp changes in elevation with the hope that the lightning will hit the higher ground. You should be far enough away from the top of the high ground to expect dissipation of the strike. At the same time you should look for protection from rock fall. A small ridge leading from the lower portion of a high cliff will be safer than the lower terrain to which a rock would roll. Wet spots in otherwise dry country sometimes attract lightning. Isolated tall trees attract lightning.

Finding an open flat site in thick woods, big enough for a tent, can be a challenge. Place your camp outside restricted use areas, and at least 100 paces from all surface water. Choose your site carefully. It is better to **bivouac** (temporarily, inconveniently camp in an unsheltered spot) in a safe location than to set up camp in a dangerous one.

Some managers of public lands want campsites to be within view of the trail, some require that they be out of sight, and some mandate that only specific sites be used. Find out which applies to the area you plan to visit.

Finding a spot for ten people in the woods requires a field reconnaissance in advance. The less steep the slope and the wider the valley, the better will be your chances of finding suitable tent sites. In northern New England, hardwood stands usually provide better openings than do softwoods or mixed growth stands.

A consideration that has only recently become important in the Northeast is that of avoiding areas frequented by moose. They do some of their traveling at night, and are large enough that their stepping on you could be very serious. Normally, they would avoid you once they hear you sleeping or they smell you. However, they might become confused if they wandered into a group of widely separated tents in their territory. For that reason, it may not be a good idea to disperse tents over a wide area. Someone else's snoring may be protecting you. Now, the reason I bring this up is not because of a known instance of trampling, but because of the nature of the beast. Moose and deer have similar behavior. Deer panic and run around in circles when they perceive that they are surrounded by as few as two hunters. They seem to lose their "game plan," and are unable to make decisions when faced with unusual contact with humans. At night a moose influenced by a slight wind shift and human scent might change direction and find in its path a new distraction as a second source of scent or noise. A third source not previously noticed could lead to confusion and panic. It is not easy to say where moose are likely to be or where they will not be. However, moose droppings, bark stripped from trees (vertical tooth marks), tracks, and heavy browsing (eating) of shrubs and trees are signs to heed.

BUILDING A FIRE

The use of wood fires has all but disappeared because of the need for advanced planning to obtain a fire permit, the convenience of stoves, and the difficulty in many locations of finding suitable wood. Added to this is the intrusion on the wilderness experience by the burned and unburned remnants of the fires. If you use a wood fire, you can minimize the impact by tending the fire until you have burned all the wood. Scatter or bury the wet ashes when you are through with the fire. If you used stones to construct a fire ring, then you should disperse these stones after use.

If you plan to have a wood fire, find out whether or not the fire wardens will issue a fire permit for places other than established campsites. If you do obtain permission for a wilderness campfire, or if you must make a fire in an emergency, then you must build the fire on mineral soil, "dirt," without decaying leaves and other organic matter. The danger associated with organic soil is the possibility of a fire burning underground in this organic material for weeks. The fire could emerge later to create a forest fire. Suitable fire building sites may dictate your campsite location. Consider gravel bars and islands in rivers ideal fire building sites, but they may not be safe places to tent in the event of heavy rains. Even a two foot wide stream high on a ridge may quickly overflow its banks when heavy rains occur.

A fire requires fuel, heat and oxygen. Water, as rain or water in the fuel, can take too much heat (heat of vaporization) away from the fire, and it will die. When you pile the wood being burned too close together, there is insufficient opportunity for the air to get to the fire. The fire will merely smolder and not burn. When the wood is too far apart there is insufficient concentration of heat, and the fire will expire. Practice fire building in wet weather. Your skill could be important to survival, if you fall into a stream in cold weather or become soaked by freezing rain. If it is under a small shelter made of bark, you can build a fire even when it is raining hard. The shelter should be big enough to provide at least six inches of air space over the wood.

When building a fire out of natural materials, it helps to know what materials are better fire starters. Some of the shrubs in the Southwest contain substantial quantities of resin, and burn with a gusto. In dry country, any dead trees or shrubs can make dry fuel. In more moist environments resinous materials are still available as cones (if dry) from some of the cone bearing (coniferous) trees. Birch bark burns readily, even when wet (it does not soak up an appreciable quantity of water). You should not have to strip the bark from living trees. Where there are living trees you probably will find trunks of dead trees. You will be surprised at how burnable the bark of a decayed white or gray birch is when you separate it from the rotten wood. The thicker the bark is the harder it is to light. Pull thin strips off old, thick bark.

Unless you have very dry wood, you will need to start with very small material and work up in size. The best material for kindling, in my opinion, is the small, dead twigs (without bark) of pine trees. If you use the smallest, and lots of them, you can get a fire going in the rain.

A candle can serve as a constant flame, which will help start a fire. Some people carry on expeditions a can of dried sawdust soaked in kerosene as a material that will greatly assist fire building in situations where it is a long distance to proper kindling. Fire starting ribbons and paste, are available, and are lighter to carry.

Just as with kindling, the best wood to use to start your fire will be softwood (coniferous) limbs that have lost their bark and which are not lying on the ground. Of course, if you split it fine enough, any wood will do. Once the fire is going, using hardwoods will reduce the amount of resinous tar that accumulates on the bottom of cooking pots. Often there is only one option.

Matches can be a big frustration when they will not light. I now carry several butane lighters, which are dependable, have a good size flame, and can burn for as long as thirty seconds without become danger-ously hot. One has to warm these lighters in a hand, armpit, or pocket before use in the winter. That is better than finding nothing on which to strike a match when it is very cold, and everything is wet or icy.

AXE USE

Modern camp cooking on a mountain usually involves a liquid fuel stove, which is quite light. Wood fires are a means to production of substantial heat, but are not practical for a party trying to cover lots of distance. Except at established campsites, where previous campers have burnt it all, one might find firewood that does not require an axe for preparation. If you must cut wood to length, a small bow saw will do the job. It is both lighter and safer than an axe. If you must have a wood fire and you have to split the only wood available, then you need an axe.

If you carry an axe, to be useful and safe it should be sharp. A dull axe is much more likely to bounce or slide out of the work and go on an unwanted errand. The axe head should taper gradually toward the cutting edge. You can test an edge to see if it is sharp by trying to shave the face of your thumbnail. If it is sharp, it will catch on the nail, and you can make a shaving. If the axe is dull, it will slide off the nail. Test the whole length of the cutting edge.

One careless blow of an axe can wreak a lot of damage. A hired man splitting firewood killed one of my aunts (two generations removed) when she was a child. She was picking up chips off the ground when his axe glanced off a chunk of firewood and hit her in the head. And I had stitches in my ankle from using a sharp axe many years ago to clear thick brush on a rainy day.

A chopper should have his hands sufficiently low that, should the axe miss the log, the follow-through would bring the axe in contact with the ground and not the chopper's body. If the chopper stands erect while chopping a log on the ground, a slip of the axe could result in a follow-through that could hit him. Whenever you are chopping, try to have your hands at about the same height as the axe head when it strikes the wood. You may have to kneel. When limbing a tree that is lying on the ground, cut only the branches on the opposite side of the trunk from you. In this case your hands must be higher than the work.

It is essential that a chopper clear all the branches around the work. Especially dangerous are those branches behind the chopper's head. If on the backswing the axe becomes caught in a branch, the branch could constrain the forward swing in such a way as to strike the back or side of the chopper's head! If I have not convinced you that this can happen, try it slowly with the sheath on the axe. Put the axe well back over your right shoulder, and catch it on a branch attached to a tree or bush behind you and to your left. Remember, I said slowly.

Splitting wood in camp is a tradition. Which way do you do it? The safest way is to provide a chopping block, place the work on the block and keep the hands low. Without a chopping block, you can lean the piece you will split against a large log lying on the ground. Again, keep the hands low. The practice of holding a piece to be split on a chopping block while the axe descends is foolhardy. The practice of bringing the hand, wood and axe down together is almost as bad. Get those hands away from the work!

In chopping through a log, progress is greatest when you can remove big chips with as few blows as possible. It pays to make the width of the start of the cut wider than the diameter of the log. After each stroke, lever the chips out as you remove the axe.

The head on your axe might be loose. If you can wiggle it, it is much too loose, and you should not use the axe. If it slides a little along the axe handle with each blow of the axe, it is dangerous. The head could come flying off in mid-swing, and strike a bystander.

How heavy should the axe be? You will usually find the axe head weight stamped on one end of the head. The axe I use for trail maintenance, carried inboard of a side pocket on my pack (in a slot for skis), is a 2 1/2 pound model with a single bit. It will adequately cut hardwood up to about six inches in diameter. I do cut larger trees with it. For larger logs and for splitting firewood, a 3 1/2 pound axe is preferable. Stronger individuals and people who split wood a lot may want a 4 1/2 or 5 pound head. For splitting heavy firewood at home, I prefer a 6 pound maul.

Because your camp may be several days' journey from a doctor's office, consider the axe a dangerous weapon and leave it at home. A bow saw is much more reasonable as a tool for hikers. If you must chop, make your decisions carefully.

WINTER CAMPING

Camping in the winter can be as much fun as in the summer; a full moon provides a splendid backdrop. You may find the trail shelters filled with snow, fully occupied, or out of reach due to slow going. They could have been recently removed. Huts and lodges are locked tight, so you will want a lightweight tent. Even if you plan to make a snow shelter, it is wise to carry a tent. There may not be enough snow.

Locate your tentsite so that it will be out of the wind even if the wind changes direction during the night. Keep in mind that you may need a bad weather escape route from your tentsite, particularly above tree line. The tentsite should not be in a potential avalanche path nor under large dead limbs. Photo 9-1 shows a tent site in the Bugaboos somewhat protected from avalanches.

One starts the preparation of a tentsite by moving snow around to make it level and by packing the snow. If the tent stakes will not hold in the loose snow, then use "dead men," which are objects, such as sticks, buried horizontally in the snow. Some people carry lightweight, drawstring bags made out of netting. They fill these with snow and bury them as dead men. Be sure that you tie the tent down well so that you will not have to crawl out to fix it when the wind is at its worst. When your tent is up, store your gear so that you will not lose it under new precipitation.

You will probably want to leave the door of your tent, or at least the vents, open. The moisture you generate will form frost on the interior of your tent. The frost on the walls will wet your sleeping bag and your clothing when you rub up against it. If the tent is large enough, you can place gear and supplies you are not using between the sleeping bag and the tent wall. Breathable nylon tents are not breathable enough to handle the moisture burden produced in the winter. Once frost forms on the nylon the fabric is essentially vapor proof.

There may seem to be no reason to use a tent when you leave the door and vents open, but there is. On a clear night, the sky, as a radiant source, has an extremely low effective temperature resulting in what is called "radiational cooling." The tent provides an artificial sky at a much warmer temperature, even if it is -20 degrees F.

When you are ready to get into your sleeping bag, take off (and replace, if you have them) your wet clothes, particularly your socks and wet undershirt. You will be amazed at how much warmer you will feel. It is far better to put on frozen outer clothes in the morning than to shiver all night trying to dry them. If you are on a multi-night outing, consider rotating socks and underwear, maintaining an "A" set and a "B" set. On days that are not too strenuous or snowy, you can dry the alternate socks and underwear inside your shirt next to your skin layer (long underwear), or on the back of your pack on sunny days. You run a greater risk of losing them when they are on the pack, however they have a chance of drying there.

If your feet are too cold in the sleeping bag, and you have no down bootees, use your down jacket. Any garment or gear placed under the foot of your sleeping bag will help keep your feet warm. If your shoulders or hips are cold because they push thin spots in the upper side of your sleeping bag, draw a sweater or other garment over them inside or outside the bag. If you find that your mid-section is coldest, you will want a shirt with long tails or something to wrap around your waist.

You will be most comfortable if you wear sufficient clothing inside your sleeping bag to keep you toasty but not sweaty. If you wear too much on a very cold night, you may experience a clammy, uncomfortable feeling of indeterminate cause. On the other hand, if you start out comfortably, you may need to add more clothing as the night progresses. This is because your blood sugar and the air temperature will drop. Keep a source of food energy handy, such as a candy bar. I find that I have to take off articles of clothing as I warm up in the sleeping bag after supper, then I have to add items as a cold night progresses.

The farther your face is outside the sleeping bag, the less moisture will condense on the bag from your breathing. Below zero, you may have difficulty keeping your nose from freezing when you keep it outside the bag. Wearing a hat (or two) or a **balaclava**[1] helps to keep your face warm. You may find that you can only keep your nose from freezing by covering it with a facemask at night. On sub-zero nights I wear a pile hat over a suede face mask that encircles my head and neck.

You will probably want to take into your sleeping bag your water bottles, inner boots, the socks you plan to wear the next day, your camera, and any food that should not freeze. All too often water bottles leak inside sleeping bags. If the cap of a water bottle has a little ice in it when you close the bottle, a leak will develop when the ice thaws. Take pains to make sure the caps are free of ice and that you have closed them tightly. It pays to check several times that the caps are tight.

Since you will have the most free time in the evening after it is dark but before you go to sleep, this is the time to melt all the snow to fill your canteens. If the water is hot, you can use the filled water bottles as hot water bottles in the sleeping bag. Even if you can get your water from a stream, you could heat it to provide that extra comfort.

You can keep warm water melted from snow in the evening from freezing overnight, if you bury the warm, covered kettle under six inches or more of snow. Make sure there are no openings in the snow that would let in cold air. You may want to mark the spot so that you will know where to dig in the morning.

In the winter, whether the weather is relatively warm or cold, the sleeping bag tends to become wet while you camp, due to:

    1) Frost on the tent,

    2) Wet clothing taken into the bag,

---

[1]A balaclava is a tube of fabric worn over the head, sealed at the top, long enough to cover the neck, with one opening for the face. A similar item with two or more openings is a face mask.

3) Snow blown or carried into the tent, and

4) Water vapor given off by the body, which subsequently condenses where the air temperature reaches the dew point at the outer shell of the bag.

The bag becomes progressively more damp each night out unless you can dry it in the sun during the day. It is possible for the bag to pick up 10 ounces of moisture or more on a four-night trip. This is a critical problem for people on extended expeditions. The recommended solution is a vapor barrier liner inside the bag and a waterproof shell outside. Unfortunately, this combination is not very comfortable unless the temperature is near zero or lower. In theory, you would like to keep the two vapor-tight shells and vary the amount of insulation between the two. I had reasonable success managing moisture on a ten day trip by using an outer bag of pile. The frost formed on the outer surface of the pile, not in the down. However, the pile bag was too heavy for backpacking (we were hauling sleds). From the moisture burden standpoint, it is safer to do extended camping at zero than at 25 degrees F.

I recommend that you place your gaiters and outer mitts under your pad at night. They will add insulation and they will thaw somewhat overnight. Sleeping bag sacks and other unused fabric items, such as wind pants, can also serve as insulation under the pad.

If it is too cold or windy to stay outside your tent and cook, crawl into your sleeping bag and cook from inside the tent with the stove just outside the downwind end. You do not want the steam inside the tent. Be sure to fill your stove outside the tent over snow you will not later melt for water. Fuel spills inside the tent are not apparent when it is very cold, because of the low vapor pressure of the fuel, and therefore are very dangerous.

Summer or winter, it takes about two hours to cook, eat, wash dishes, pack, break camp and get on the trail. You can cut this time nearly in half, if you can get along without using a fire or stove. This means having a cold breakfast or using a thermos.

One summer Les, David and I camped without a tent at about 10,000 feet on a ridge on the northeast side of Mt. Rainier. It was pleasant weather and the undercast was magnificent. We slept on snow in the shelter of the extension of a very steep west-facing wall. It did not take long for us to figure out that the nearby rock was volcanic in origin. The prevailing wind from the west swept up that wall carrying with it a fine pumice dust, which got into everything. It was in our eyes, mouths, sleeping bags, the food we ate, everything. Now, I look to see whether or not the snow has a covering of inorganic debris, whether small particles or fallen stones.

WASTE DISPOSAL

In the summer, you can dispose of excrement by burying it and toilet paper under soil. In the winter (with a snow cover), and on snow in the summer, any disposal in the snow is temporary. There is essentially no organic decay of the waste at freezing temperatures, and the cold preserves the pathogens. Some National Park regulations require that hikers and climbers on snow covered peaks carry out excrement in special plastic bags. This is not onerous in that transport is mostly down hill, and at cool temperatures there is not much of an odor problem. A friend who works in the woods says he believes that excrement buried in snow dissipates so that little remains after the snow melts. In order for it to dissipate, the excrement must be on the snow or ground surface during spring rains. Rain water then carries particles of the excrement downhill, and will pollute any downstream water in the spring of the year. During my winter hiking on the Appalachian Trail I have made an effort to camp at shelters with privies. There seem to be only two other proper alternatives:
1) Dig down through the snow cover to the ground for burial in soil (this assumes that the ground is not frozen, which is often the case where the snow cover is a foot or more), or
2) Carry it out to the trailhead for disposal in a toilet (the plastic is solid waste).

In summer, leaving waste and toilet paper on the ground surface is unwise, because of the potential for flies to carry disease, and because of the aesthetic degradation.

EMERGENCY SHELTERS

Shelters (tents and lean-tos) provide protection from one or more of the following:
1) Wind,
2) Precipitation,

3) Wind blown particles (sand, pumice or hail),

4) Insects,

5) Radiational cooling by a clear night sky, and

6) Wandering rodents.

In the summer you can make an emergency shelter, which only has to keep rain off your sleeping area, from ponchos, sheet polyethylene or a nylon fly (tarp).

Originally a **bivouac sack** was a coated fabric bag meant for use as a one person emergency tent. Sometimes these are big enough for two people. It was discovered that in survival conditions people who share body heat in such a sack do better. Now a bivouac sack can mean a fabric shelter large enough for a party. You can use a tent without poles, or you can design a bag specifically for bivouacs. The one I constructed has a length of seven feet and a circumference of about fifteen feet (three widths of 60 inch material). I used drawstrings to close the ends. It weighs about two pounds, and will provide a closed emergency shelter for six people (seated). Smaller models would accommodate fewer people. Construct such sacks of lightweight coated nylon cloth (1.5 or 2 oz.). The shared body heat in such a shelter is greater than you might think, and is critical in survival situations.

In the winter a snow structure could provide shelter from wind and snow, but might not be water tight. You could place a waterproof covering on top of the snow structure.

To build an igloo from blocks of snow requires two people, at least two hours of daylight, old compacted snow, or rained on frozen snow, and some engineering skill. An alternative construction method, suitable for non-compacted snow and requiring a minimum of engineering, involves

1) Making a pile of snow somewhat higher than the desired igloo,

2) Waiting for the pile of snow to consolidate, and

3) Digging out the inside of the pile.

The time for the snow to consolidate will depend on the moisture content and the shape of the snow particles. Wait at least 30 minutes with heavy, structured snow. If the snow was very loose when you made the pile, then you should wait longer. The sooner you begin excavation the greater is the risk that there will be a collapse.

You can dig a snow cave in a snow bank without having to wait for snow to settle, but you will need snow that is sufficiently deep. Sometimes, the snow is deep enough next to a downed tree. Unless the temperature is really low, you will want waterproof clothing while digging out the snow cave or igloo.

Some hiking authorities have found that a snow trench offers the fastest shelter for each individual. They recommend digging a narrow trench (about 20 inches wide, 3 feet deep and 8 feet long), covering it first with branches and then with snow. The trench should be open only at one end, the entrance. An insulating pad will make a mattress and floor. The trench can be wider than 20 inches at the floor, but it is difficult to bridge when wider at the top. Where the snow is not 3 feet deep, you can pile snow high and dig it out later as with the loose snow igloo.

Photo 9-2 shows a snow trench built in about an hour. The icy layers of snow under the surface were so tough that a steel shovel was necessary. It might have been possible to break these layers with a boot, but it would have taken longer. There were trees under the snow that constrained the entrance.

Igloos, caves and trenches will be warmer if the floor is higher than the entrance. Warm air rises and will be more effectively trapped, when the entrance is lower than the living space (shelf).

All snow structures will settle as time passes. If you are going to use your snow shelter for more than a couple of days, allow extra height during construction.

All occupied snow shelters will develop an impermeable, glazed surface on the interior. They must have adequate ventilation with openings that will not be blocked by new or wind blown snow, snow dropped from tree branches, or a collapsed snow structure. A college student died in her sleep when snow fell off a tree during the night and blocked the entrance to her individual snow shelter. Mountaineers have died when snow drifts blocked snow cave entrances. It is prudent to poke at least one hole in the roof of a snow shelter, which will contribute to air circulation. The hole does not have to be right in the center over your head.

The tool usually used to make snow shelters is a lightweight, collapsible shovel made of aluminum or plastic. Mine is an emergency shovel made for use in a car; it has a plastic scoop. I have substituted an aluminum tube for the original tubular handle made of steel. You can use a snowshoe in an emergency. You may be able to find a shovel that clamps onto an ice axe. A plastic sled is useful as a mining cart, particularly when someone is available outside the snow cave to empty the sled.

Do not underestimate how long a snow shelter will take to build or how wet the builder will become. You will have a better knowledge of the limitations and problems of snow shelter construction, if you practice building them.

Regardless of how cold it is outside, the temperature inside a properly built, inhabited igloo or snow cave is likely to be around freezing. The result could be that clothing and gear will become wetter in a snow shelter than they would in a tent.

You can best learn camping skills by trying a little bit new at a time and by trying these new experiences in a controlled way. Build your first igloo at a time and place where it is not critical to your survival. Sleep out in a shed or backyard to test your sleeping bag at low temperatures. Choose a day when you are not in the wilderness to practice building a fire in the rain. Do understand that all of the practice you undertake contributes to the knowledge base needed for making good decisions. ❄

MOUNTAINEERING

It is the purpose of this chapter to discuss the hazards of some mountaineering activities. The only skill I will talk about at length is snowshoeing, because this is an activity that beginners are likely to undertake without instruction. Here, too, there are hazards, such as brook crossings, spruce traps, and avalanche slopes. The principal message of this chapter is that mountaineering, particularly that which starts out as just a hike, involves skills needed to overcome obstacles such as glaciers, steep ice, and steep rock. In order to understand and recognize the dangers, you need instruction, which is best obtained through a structured program. Remember, when you reach that technical terrain, you need knowledge and skill as the basis for making sound decisions

A LOOK AT TECHNICAL SKILLS

In serious mountain climbing you are likely to climb roped, either continuously or with belays. However there is no benefit to the others on the rope, if you do not know how to belay.

BELAYING: Belays are important to learn, since you never know when you will need to use one to help someone else:
1) Cross an unexpected icy stretch,
2) Descend slabs dangerous when wet,
3) Climb a simple pitch that he or she is mentally unprepared to do without the rope, etc.

While current practice in rock climbing involves use of a belaying device, the quicker body belay is often more useful for mountaineering. A belayer holds the rope in such a way that he or she can hold a fall by the person climbing. The rope passing around the belayer's body provides the friction necessary to stop a fall. Usually, the belayer is anchored. The belayer *must* be ready at all times to instantly react to a fall by the climber. This means that the belayer must keep his or her control hand around the rope at all times. Usually the belayer is securely tied into anchors so that he or she is not pulled off the face by the other person's fall.

Often the climber and the belayer cannot see each other and can barely hear each other. So, they need a set of signals with which they can communicate without any misunderstanding. Words like "slack" and "rope" must have unmistakable meaning to both climbers.

Appropriate instruction in belaying includes practice in catching the fall of a heavy weight dropped vertically, usually from a pulley attached to a tree limb. During all body belaying you should wear gloves, and at least one heavy shirt, to avoid the serious rope burns that could occur.

ROCK CLIMBING: Do not assume that rock climbing on Eastern metamorphic rock is anything like climbing Western sedimentary peaks. What you can ski in May could involve a rock climb in late June. Rock climbing skills learned in the South might not prepare you for the wind-chill you might encounter on a ledge in the North.

Bear in mind that rock climbing is inherently dangerous. The sport of rock climbing takes as its focus pushing the limits to see how far you can go before falling off the rock face. On the other hand, learning to ascend less demanding pitches teaches you what kinds of moves will help you over the rock when the technique is a means to reaching a summit. Even then, the temptation to push the limits creeps into the picture. Your decision as to how far to go must be based, not only on the level of rock climbing ability required, but also, on the weather, opportunities to descend, the ability of the people with you, time considerations, and the implications of a fall.

RAPPELLING: A rappel is a controlled descent of a stationary (static) rope. Do not try it without instruction. It looks easy; done wrong, it could result in a fatal fall. You can accomplish control of your descent by wrapping the rope around the body in a figure eight ("body wrap") so that there is sufficient friction, or by means of a mechanical device that creates the friction. In either case the control hand holds the rope entering the friction zone and can control the amount of friction. If a rappeler "freaks out" in the middle of a rappel, he or she is likely to fall or be frozen at that one place unable to proceed. It is appropriate to belay all beginners. Experienced climbers sometimes are struck by rocks and lose control, or rappel off the end of their rope. Either could be fatal. Please use good judgment, and do not try rappels without instruction and a belay.

GLISSADING: A glissade is a slide in a standing, sitting or squatting position down a snow-covered slope without the aid of skis. Photo 10-1 shows climbers glissading in a squatting and a standing position. Both have their ice axes ready to execute a self-arrest. It can be great fun, and it's the kind of activity beginners are tempted to try. Ideal conditions are those in which the snow is not frozen so hard that one cannot brake with feet or an ice axe. On the other hand, it is not possible to slide unless the snow is rather firm. If the snow is soft, you may not slide unless all the snow goes with you.

The danger in glissading is that you may not be able to stop at the end of the smooth snow or when you encounter some other danger. A common mistake is to glissade right down to the rocks at the end of a snow field and then not be able to stop. The dangerous condition may be out of view when you start the glissade. The condition could be a change in snow texture to a very icy slope. This can occur where snow covered an exposed ledge and water running over the ledge changed the snow to ice. It could be the change to a much steeper slope.

A tragic example of unforeseen consequences will certainly make the point. In 1966 a group of us climbed Symmetry Spire in Grand Teton National Park in June. The descent route is down a steep (close to 40 degree slope) gully that was snow filled at the time. Photo 10-1 shows two of the group members descending that gully. The Park Rangers warned us that holes might open up in the snow, because of a brook below the snow. We were able to execute skiing turns while doing a standing glissade, because the hard snow had a thawed surface only an inch deep. We did not see any holes. A week later a climber descending the same gully found himself in a slow moving, wet snow slide. He could not get out of it. He and the snow slid into a hole and down to the brook. The heavy snow trapped him and blocked the flow of the brook. He drowned.

I recommend that you glissade only on slopes you have ascended and examined and which have a very safe run out. You need an ice axe for control purposes, and you need to know how to self-arrest before you try glissades.

You can do a standing glissade on steep slopes on snowshoes in soft snow by shuffling the feet to keep the snowshoes on top of the snow. You will have to keep your weight well back on the snowshoes. If much directional control were possible, we could call it skiing. The pitch of the slope has to be rather steep for this type of glissade and soft snow on steep slopes could avalanche. I recommend that you only attempt snowshoe glissades on wooded slopes.

SELF-ARREST: A self-arrest is the technique of slowing or stopping either a glissade or an out-of-control descent of a snow or ice covered slope. You do this by assuming a prone position belly down with one hand gripped very firmly over the head of the ice axe and the other well down on the shaft. You force the pick of the ice axe into the snow or ice with all the weight you can bring to bear on the axe. You also use your feet. The difficulty in self-arrest on steep slopes is that you must apply much of the stopping force through the pick of the ice axe. You have to transfer this to the body through the arms. It is like trying to do a chin up on your ice axe. Some people have lost a grip on the axe. As instructed in the military, "**DO NOT DROP YOUR WEAPON!**" You must exert a great deal of force to keep the axe from sliding over the head where you cannot use it effectively. In that position, it is not possible to get your weight to bear on the head of the axe. You should try chin-ups on your ice axe to obtain an idea of the force required on steep slopes. Only on steep, firm snow can one practice stopping a slide.

It is possible to fall so as to slide out of control on your back, feet first, down the slope. Yes, it is also possible to slide downhill on your back with your head first. You need instruction and practice in the correct method to use to arrest such slides.

There is, of course, some danger that any one of the sharp surfaces of the ice axe will injure you in an uncontrolled slide. For this reason you should hold the axe with a steel-like grip to minimize the possible motion of the axe relative to your body.

CRAMPONING: If the snow or ice slope is sufficiently steep that you could slip and slide out of control, then you need crampons and an ice axe along with the appropriate instruction.

Whenever you place your crampons on the ice, whether in the use of front points or bottom points, placement should occur with vigor. There should be nothing tentative about crampon placement. Tentative placement could result in a tentative hold. One commonly sees an inexperienced ice climber kicking the ice repeatedly with blows which lack conviction. You can feel an insecure placement, but you usually cannot obtain a good placement with these little kicks.

Beginners tend to want to keep their feet level when traversing an ice slope. This means that only the uphill points of the crampons support your weight. We call this **edging**. I have seen a friend slide several hundred feet down **boiler plate** (hard snow, sometimes with an icy surface) as a result of this improper technique. Always plant all the spikes, unless you are front pointing.

Front pointing, using the front points of the crampons, which you drive perpendicularly into the ice, allows you to ascend directly up ice steeper than about forty degrees. It is also a technique that you can employ on steeper, hard packed snow. What becomes very important as the gradient increases is the quality of the protection provided by the two tools in the climber's hands. Specialized ice tools have evolved that are designed for this purpose.

There can be such secure holds when front pointing that they build overconfidence. While the quality of the climber's technique might not change, the ice could change in a matter of a few feet. Ice can change from a soft, wet, new ice to a flaky, brittle, exfoliating ice that comes off in layers. The ice can become too thin to hold a tool, an ice screw or front points. Find a mentor and responsible instruction.

GLACIERS AND CREVASSE RESCUE: All parties should be roped when walking on glaciers. They should be wearing crampons, have an ice axe in hand, and have prusik loops or ascenders attached to the rope in anticipation of a crevasse self-rescue. They should also have on gloves and, perhaps, more clothing than they might otherwise wear. If you fall into a crevasse with skis or snowshoes on, you will be handicapped in your self-rescue.

All party members must be prepared to execute a self-arrest immediately when someone on the rope falls into a crevasse. Otherwise, you might be pulled into the crevasse. If the fallen climber can take his weight off the rope, the self-arrest climber(s) can get into a belay position with the ice axe used as the protection (anchor).

If you fall into a crevasse, the other person(s) on the rope will quite possibly be unable to pull you out of the void. You will find that the conditions are much colder than they were on the surface of the glacier. You will have to get your feet into prusik slings and climb the rope using the prusiks.

You might land in a crevasse upside down with your pack weight preventing you from righting yourself. In this event it would be nice to have a way of getting out of your pack without dropping it. If you are prepared with a line from the climbing rope and attached to the pack, you can take the pack off and ascend with it below you. Obtain instruction.

HIGH ANGLE SNOW: If you could not readily stop a slide down the slope by a self-arrest, or, if there is no safe run out at the bottom of the slope, then travel roped and belay each other. Belay anchors in snow consist of:

1) An ice axe or **picket** (a long thin object like a stake) driven into the snow,
2) A **fluke** (metal plate with wire sling) driven into the snow and rigged to drive deeper into the snow under load,
3) A buried object (called a **dead man**) and
4) A **bollard** (a snow or ice structure or circular excavation around which the rope is placed).

High angle snow is inherently dangerous, because of the threat of avalanche and the possibility of sliding on the snow until rocks are encountered. Consult with avalanche experts, and obtain instruction in the techniques used on high angle snow. It is very enlightening to do some testing of snow anchors with a tension measuring device.

SNOWSHOEING

My mental picture of snowshoeing involves putting one foot in front of the other in soft snow on moderate terrain. However, I have no trouble changing that picture to one of frightening aspect. If the terrain is covered with large boulders, changes to ice, involves serious spruce traps, includes stream crossings, or has lots of blowdowns, then there is the possibility of falling or becoming trapped. For this reason, I recommend that you not snowshoe alone.

METAL FRAMED SNOWSHOES: About 1970 aluminum framed snowshoes became an option. While somewhat heavier than traditional snowshoes of the same size, these snowshoes have become the usual choice. Most people now use aluminum framed snowshoes substantially smaller in area than the older wooden snowshoes. This is fine under most snow conditions. However, in very soft powder, the smaller snowshoes will sink right through to the underlying, denser snow. I have even found myself shuffling along without the snowshoes coming to the surface. There is less work involved when you do not sink. The fraction of the time when the snow is that soft, and you do sink deeply, is less later in the season.

Metal framed snowshoes do break, and they will not withstand continued abuse on the rocks one commonly encounters above tree line in winter.

WOODEN FRAMED SNOWSHOES: My reason for discussing wooden snowshoes is that they offer a slightly lighter, larger alternative to the metal framed snowshoe. This is desirable when faced with deep powder. Snowshoes have been made in a wide variety of sizes, shapes and materials. Traditional snowshoes have steam-bent wooden frames with rawhide stringing. They come with and without tails. The tails make maneuvering in thick woods more difficult, but they also help keep the back of the snowshoe from lifting off the snow with each step. Keeping the back ends down is desirable, because it helps the snowshoe clear itself of the snow that accumulates on top. Having tails that fall helps prevent the toe of the snowshoe from catching on the upper layers of snow with the resulting loss of balance of the snowshoer. The most common styles with tails are the Michigan (or Maine), the Bear Paw, the Beavertail, and the Pickerel See Figure 10-1. The Alaskan snowshoe is appropriate for deep powder and relatively flat terrain. A smaller snowshoe will sink more deeply, and require you to do more work.

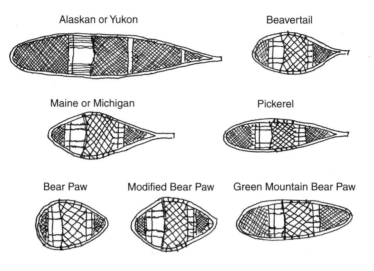

Figure 10-1: Styles Of Wooden-Framed Snowshoes

Wooden snowshoes are also available without tails. Bear Paw, Modified Bear Paw, and Green Mountain Bear Paw snowshoes were the most common styles used by mountain hikers in the East in the past. Snowshoes without tails are easier to maneuver in thick woods, and without tails it is easier to kick steps up a steep slope.

Thirteen inches is the maximum snowshoe width that you are likely to find comfortable for a long hike. Even at that width, you will have to waddle a bit. When you take long steps with snowshoes of modest length, you can place them more or less in front of each other. It is even more important to not have snowshoes that are too wide, if they are very long like the Alaskan style.

The fore and aft distance between crosspieces on wooden snowshoes should not be less than 14 inches, unless the people who wear them have short feet.

Bear Paw and Modified Bear Paw snowshoes are usually 30 to 36 inches long. Michigan and Pickerel snowshoes are usually 42 to 48 inches long.

The most critical failure of any snowshoes occurs when the principal transverse webbing under the ball of the foot fails. This is most likely to occur when one jumps down from a ledge, or when one jumps across a gap or stream. They were not built for this abuse. Rawhide is particularly weak when wet. It becomes wet when snowshoeing at temperatures above freezing.

I recommend urethane varnish or spar varnish for wooden snowshoes and rawhide lacing, because it stands up well in wet conditions.

After World War II, neoprene coated nylon stringing became available. This material stands up well in abrasion resistance. It does not lose any strength when wet; however it is somewhat heavier than rawhide.

Regardless of the material of which the snowshoes are made, the heavier you and your pack are, the larger the snowshoes should be. They should be larger for a given snow condition in order to reduce, the amount of work that accompanies sinking into deep snow. You do not want to work harder than the people you are with, so do not try to use smaller snowshoes. On the other hand Alaskan snowshoes, which are about six feet long, are impractical (too long) for use on Eastern trails or in Eastern woods.

EMERGENCY SNOWSHOES: Almost any flat object will do as long as you can rig bindings that hinge as do those on traditional snowshoes. I recommend that you cut for each snowshoe two large, bushy softwood branches (spruce or fir) about four feet long. It helps if the inside branches have some curvature (place the convex side toward the opposite snowshoe). Tie the two butts together at about a 30 degree angle. About 18 and 24 inches back from the point, tie two crosspieces on top to support the foot. You want the boot toe to pivot around the forward crosspiece. Tie the boot to this crosspiece in a manner simulating a snowshoe harness (over the toe, back around the back of the boot, around the ankle and back to the crosspiece, but be inventive). See Photo 10-2 in which webbing serves for the harness. You should find walking with these on deep snow easier than without, but you will have to take long strides, and you may have to trim the edges of the inside branches.

SNOWSHOE BINDINGS: If you have trouble with your snowshoes not staying aligned with your boot (your heel hits the side of the snowshoe), look at the toe of the boot. If the toe is slipping over to one side of the binding toe-piece, it will cause this misalignment problem. To correct this problem, use a wider boot or rig the binding so that it is narrower.

The second way in which snowshoe bindings can be frustrating is when the strap around the back of the foot falls down and the binding comes completely off the boot. I offer three solutions:

1) Make that strap long enough so that it can make a full turn around the ankle (You may have to buckle an additional strap onto the one that is too short.),

2) Sew a loop of webbing low on the backside of your boot, or gaiter, through which you can pass the strap, or

3) Place a strap over the top of the foot, which you attach to the strap around the back of your foot.

These attachments will ensure that you will not lose your snowshoe down a steep slope, if your toe does work its way out of the toepiece.

If the toe of the boot works its way out of the binding, make sure the toe-piece is not too wide, and that the boot is not too far back in the binding. Also try to tighten the toe-piece around the boot. Some plastic, winter boots taper so much toward the front that they are difficult to keep in traditional snowshoe bindings. If the boot is too far forward in the binding, it will hit on the forward crosspiece.

SNOWSHOE CREEPERS: For mountain hiking, you should affix to your snowshoes some sort of claw, crampon or creeper on the bottom under the foot. It has been the practice to attach a half of a surplus army crampon, with the ring arms bent flat, to each traditional snowshoe. These were tied on with nylon cord, and they were heavy. See Photo 10-3. Now, the aluminum framed snowshoes have bindings that have the claws attached to the bottom. The creeper, attached to the foot in this way, bears on whatever supports the foot, regardless of what the snowshoe is doing. These claws come in a variety of sizes and shapes. The most useful have points that stick down an inch and a half. See Photo 10-3. These points help a lot when ascending steep trails and when crossing icy patches above tree line. They are not an adequate substitute for boot crampons when crossing sloping ice.

TECHNIQUE: Snowshoeing is very difficult unless the snowshoe hinges freely about the ball of the foot. This is the crux in snowshoeing. When you pick your foot up, the tail of the snowshoe should drop down until the snowshoe is close to vertical (less than 45 degrees from the vertical). There are several reasons why it might not:

1) The boot may be too far forward and it may catch on the forward end of the toe opening,

2) The boot may be too wide for the toe opening (use a narrower boot or obtain bigger snowshoes), or

3) The binding strap that goes over the toe may be attached to the snowshoe too far back (it should attach to the main cross webbing at the aft end of the toe hole).

Do not underestimate the energy required to pack snow on snowshoes. When the snow is soft and the trail goes uphill a lot of work is involved! However more energy is required to bare boot the same trail. Once the trail has been packed, travel on snowshoes still remains easier than bare booting over the same packed trail.

Going uphill on snowshoes, if there is a choice, the longer and less steep route will actually be faster than the direct route. Uphill snowshoeing is hard work, particularly if the new snow is quite deep. You will want to take turns packing trail. One hundred steps are enough for someone in good shape; others should try fewer. It is appropriate for the person who is second in line to do the counting too.

It is easier to go up steep slopes with aluminum framed snowshoes parallel to the snow surface than is possible with traditional snowshoes. In part this is due to the significant curvature at the front of these snowshoes. The curvature and narrow width allow the foot to sink farther into the snow than most of the remainder of the snowshoe, and the foot is on somewhat of a compacted step. Wooden snowshoes are flatter and do not provide as much of a step. When these steps harden due to rain and subsequent freezing, the snowshoer must take care to place the foot on the high points in order to ensure contact of the snowshoe creepers with the snow.

When the going becomes quite steep, it is very difficult to lift the snowshoe high enough to place it both uphill and on top of the snow, sometimes a matter of three feet. Facing the slope and kicking steps with the snowshoe allows one to ascend rather steep snow. This is tough on the snowshoes. It is easier to accomplish with snowshoes that are quite flat, such as the bear paw style. However, you can kick steps even with snowshoes that turn up as much as do the common aluminum framed models.

You can use ski poles with moderate sized baskets to assist yourself up steep going. They are more help than an ice axe, once you become used to where to place them. They certainly help you keep your balance on steep going, in high winds, and when crossing streams. They can also be of help in retrieving a snowshoe stuck below the snow and under a branch or rock. Often you can retrieve one end by bearing down on the other end while picking up the foot.

I recommend to you Gene Prater's book entitled *Snowshoeing*. Again, I remind you that you can fall into traps that are very difficult to get out of when wearing snowshoes. It is advisable to not travel alone.

Snowshoeing can be a wonderful means to practical travel on a mountain, as long as the snow is neither too steep nor too hard and there are no crevasses. When there is no snow or when conditions on the mountain change to those unsuitable for snowshoes, you may need technical skills. You need instruction as to the safe way to climb, and you need to understand the limitations of your skills and of the techniques. I encouraged you to seek out schools and workshops run by mountain clubs as a source of instruction in all the techniques pertinent to mountain climbing. You cannot properly learn about placing ice protection without doing it in the field. You need substantial experience with crampons and ice axe before relying on them where there is exposure to a possible fall. Each skill extends the type of terrain you can handle. Each experience with that skill provides you with knowledge that is crucial to making decisions about whether or not to continue on the next mountain. ❄

CLOTHING AND EQUIPMENT

Mountain hikers have much to fear regarding hypothermia. It can be insidious and malignant. Proper clothing is the primary defense.

INSULATION AND MOISTURE

You expect clothing worn outdoors to:
1) Keep you warm,
2) Provide ventilation to carry away moisture produced by your skin,
3) Be functional for hiking, and
4) Keep precipitation from reaching your inner clothing layers, since clothing is more comfortable and provides much more insulation when it is dry.

The lightest insulation is a vacuum; the next lightest is a dead air space. Any material that supplies dead air spaces, or even slows down air flow, could serve as insulation. Steel wool and mouse nests would each do the job, but they both have undesirable properties. A windbreaker over a sweater is the common solution. Spruce branch tips inside a fabric container could provide emergency insulation, as inside a poncho around an injured person. Large dead air spaces do not work, however, because convection currents become established which efficiently carry body heat away (as in older style, tubular type air mattresses). The insulating value of most materials increases with thickness. Many layers of clothing are desirable because of the trapped air spaces between layers and the possibility of adjusting, incrementally, the amount of insulation provided by the clothing.

Cotton clothing is inappropriate in the mountains, whether it is as jeans, tee shirts, underwear, shirts, or socks. When cotton is wet, it not only does not keep you warm, it efficiently carries away your body heat by conduction. The garment clings to you and holds enough water to make a good heat conductor causing significant heat loss.

Two materials, wool and down, have especially suited the hiker's needs for hundreds of years. Wool conducts less heat than cotton when wet, keeping the body warmer. Down has the best thickness-to-weight ratio. Both materials breathe readily.

While wool and down do their jobs well, synthetic substitutes have come along which have even more benefits. In place of wool, polypropylene, acrylic and dacron fabrics have been developed which provide insulation, but which will also hold less moisture. Manufacturers make the claim for polypropylene and dacron underwear that any moisture present will be wicked away to outer layers eventually. The benefit is that the wet fabric will not chill the body as much as wool would, with its greater burden of moisture. The synthetic fabric will dry faster. Moths do not care much for the synthetics. Acrylic, dacron, and polypropylene garments are soft, and do not scratch or cause itching like wool. Synthetic pile provides thicker insulation than the usual woven fabric. It will not collapse as down will when wet. However, a pile garment will not compress into as small a space as a down item would, making it bulkier to carry.

The moisture that plagues the hiker originates in five ways:
1) Sweat,
2) Precipitation which falls on you (including snow which melts on your clothing),
3) Water which you walk in or sit in,
4) Vapor given off by the body (called **insensible perspiration**), and
5) **Respired moisture** (moisture vapor in your breath).

Going slowly, or taking off enough clothing to reduce the skin temperature, will minimize sweat and insensible perspiration. While some people recommend "hiking cold," becoming too cold can be insidious, particularly late in the day. It can result in torn muscles. Beginners often wear too much clothing, because they have not learned that the slightest perspiration is a signal to take something off before the inner layers become soaked. One commonly sees others wearing clothing that was appropriate earlier in the day, but which has become too much clothing. Now they are sweating hard.

Waterproof materials do the best job of holding off mist and heavy rain, but they do not allow moisture coming from the skin to escape. The result is that the inside of your raingear can become as wet as if it leaked badly. Avoid water*proof* clothing except for intentional vapor barriers, raingear, ponchos, and boots (for some purposes). Loose, light garments of waterproof or water resistant material can provide air circulation to carry off the moisture vapor. Air vents with water shedding flaps increase ventilation.

Snow falling on your shoulders melts and runs down your back. You may want to devise a small poncho to keep snow from lodging there. It helps to use a ski pole or an ice axe to knock snow off branches before brushing against them along a narrow trail. Wearing outer garments made of materials to which the snow is less likely to stick will help, such as nylon and other fabrics made slippery by special coatings[1]. It pays to keep snow brushed off clothing. You will find that at temperatures below 15 degrees F. you will have far less of a problem with snow melting on your clothing.

At 100% humidity, with the body and the ambient air at the same temperature, the air cannot absorb more moisture from the body, such as insensible perspiration. However, at low outside air temperatures, the relative humidity is lowered when the air is warmed inside clothing. If that air takes on more moisture from the body, you would like to remove it from your clothing before it cools and reaches the dew point (see Chapter 6).

The moisture that collects in boots and socks, and the frost which forms inside your parka and tent in cold weather, results from moisture vapor cooled sufficiently to reach the dew point. In cold weather

---

[1]Most non-waterproof garments intended to repel precipitation have a water repellent coating that makes them slippery. I will discuss this further under "Rain Gear vs. Wind Gear."

there are two ways to deal with the problem of wet socks. The first solution is to wear plastic bags as a vapor barrier, or you can wear vapor barrier socks, over a light pair of socks but inside the heavier socks. Inside the barrier, conditions are damp, but the outer socks stay drier and insulate better. Moist feet, however, are more prone to blistering. A second solution is to ventilate the vapor laden air and get rid of it before the air reaches the dew point. Mukluks made of porous leather or fabric (also the upper part of snowmobile boots) may serve this function, but they are too flexible for you to wear with crampons. For winter use, parkas and wind pants should have porosity and zippers to permit controlled ventilation (armpits, bottom and top of pant legs, full front jacket openings).

Even porous fabric will no longer convey moisture vapor once frost has formed on it. In cold weather you should expect some frost to form where the air reaches the dew point inside the outer layer, which is usually a parka. You should also expect to put on that parka with the frost still in it, after a winter overnight, but it will still help to keep you warm. You can minimize the frost in your parka by keeping your skin cool (by taking off layers).

If you use pile as your outer layer in very cold weather (when it is not snowing or very windy), you may find that the pile will become filled with frost, some of which you can brush off the surface. If there is snow in the air (falling or blowing), the pile may accumulate it rather than shedding it. If you put a shell over a pile garment full of frost, the frost may melt resulting in significant wetting of all your clothes. Therefore, in snowy weather it is a good idea to keep the shell on and vary the number of layers underneath.

Respired moisture can rapidly wet the inside of a cooled container. Tempting as it may be, putting your nose into your sleeping bag will make the bag moisture laden and thermally inefficient. This is because the dew point is reached near the outer surface. Avoid putting a scarf over your face when you are hiking, if it allows the breath to exit into your clothing. Make sure your face mask is not causing your breath to wet your clothing.

At all times it is important to adjust (minimize) the number of layers of clothing as you hike so as to keep as dry as possible while still keeping warm. The flip side of this is the need to be aware of when you cool down, and to put on layers. When the wind picks up, when you stop for lunch, and when you start walking downhill instead of uphill, see each of these changes as a signal that you need to add a layer.

At 10 degrees F., with light winds and no snow in the air, you might start hiking by wearing five layers on your upper body. After warming up you may be down to two layers while going uphill with a pack. Expect that the layer next to your body will be somewhat damp, but not soaked. The outer layer may also be slightly damp. The layers in your pack should be dry.

On a multiple-night winter trip you cannot carry enough clothing to provide the luxury of a change to dry clothing each night. You have to manage the layering carefully, and dry the damp layers by wearing them during moderate exercise. Wet snowfall and rain make this very difficult. The most dangerous conditions you can encounter involve a sudden drop in temperature and high winds (a cold front) after a soaking rain or a wet snowstorm. I could argue that you should carry more clothing (a change of clothing) under warmer winter conditions, since it is possible to keep your clothing much dryer in a cold snowstorm than in a warmer snow or rain. On the other hand, at temperatures around freezing, and with light winds, you may be comfortable hiking with only one layer on top. If you can keep everything else relatively dry, you will not need a complete change of clothing.

CLOTHING LAYERS

In order to better understand the function of specific items, note in the list on the next page the clothing I wear under a series of conditions. Clearly, individuals differ both as to what they have available to them in the way of clothing and in what they find comfortable wearing after warming up by hiking. The items listed below are only suggested. Make a chart and record what you have been comfortable wearing under various conditions. Probably, your first inclination will be to wear too much.

Table 11-1 — Table Of Clothing Selections For Various Windchill Conditions

WCT	UPHILL	DOWNHILL	INACTIVE
60	1	1	2
45	2	2	4
29	3	3-4	6-8
13	4-5	5	9
-2	5-6	6-7	9
-18	6	6-7	9
-34	6-7	7	10
-49	7	8	10
-64	8	8	10

WHAT THE NUMBERS MEAN: The first column provides the windchill temperature in degrees F. The other numbers refer to the clothing selections below.

1 - Shorts and polypro top.
2 - Shorts and long sleeved shirt over a polypro top.
3 - Shorts and polypro bottoms, or long pants, and shirt over polypro top.
4 - Long underwear tops and bottoms, heavy pants, shirt, and, possibly, a shell.
5 - Add a parka shell, hat, gaiters, and mittens.
6 - Add a sweater or pile pullover.
7 - Add wind pants and mitten shells.
8 - Add another sweater or pullover, face mask and goggles.
9 - Add a down jacket (or equivalent), perhaps in place of the parka.
10 - I get into my sleeping bag, if in camp.

I was comfortable (without shivering) sitting for an extended period at the end of the day wearing category 6 (without the face mask) when the WCT was 0 degrees. Refer to the Windchill graph in Chapter 4, and consider the implications for survival in a summer storm without all this clothing. In the summer the temperature would be somewhere between 20 and 60 degrees F. and the wind speed might be between 40 and 60 miles per hour.

The author now wears and carries, or uses, the following in winter: polypropylene (or equivalent) long sleeved turtleneck and long underwear bottoms, mid-weight polypropylene shirt with a few buttons at the front of the neck (Wallace Berry style), acrylic shirt, light acrylic sweater, light pile pullover, heavy pile pullover (in place of down jacket), mountain parka with taffeta lining, wool pants, breathable, lined wind pants, and insulated gaiters

A common layering system involves wearing wind pants over long underwear bottoms and hiking shorts, with pile pants you can add under the wind pants when it becomes cold. This is a fine combination of layers, except that you have to unzip the wind pants most of the way down the sides in order to get the pile pants under them. Both layers have to have separating zippers. Do you know how frustrating it is when your pants are down and you have a stuck zipper? Most people vary the layers on the top half of their body by adding layers under their parka shell, but these can be layers that do not have zippers. Parkas have zippers, but they also have backup closure systems consisting of snaps or Velcro®.

Consider renting or borrowing equipment and clothing before buying, in order to become familiar with the problem features of each item. Shop as long as you can. Try out as many styles as possible, and choose carefully. Talk with leaders. Ask friends. Consider making your own clothing. Be wary about what salespeople tell you. Many do not have substantial experience, and some believe their choices are the best for you. Both *Outside* and *Backpacker* magazines include discussions of equipment either monthly or in an annual equipment issue. Use the latter and catalogs to compare competing brands. Shop a lot. You may spend more than $2000 for your clothing and equipment, so it pays to not make hasty choices.

I will mention again for emphasis that cold feet and hands are not divorced from what is happening to the whole body. Reduction of the heat loss from any part of the body contributes to the welfare of the remainder. Therefore, putting on a hat helps to keep your feet from becoming colder. Do not let your feet become cold. Add clothes at the timberline and at the summit before you become chilled. Once the feet are cold it takes a long time to rewarm them. Similarly, if your hands become cold, it is a signal that the whole body is cooling. Conversely, when your hands begin to sweat, you may need to take off more than your mittens. Be alert! Make the right decisions!

SPECIFIC CLOTHING ITEMS

BOOTS: Boots are the most critical item of your outfit. Choose them for fit, warmth, traction, ankle support, and protection from the sloppy stuff. Break them in before a long hike. I suggest Vibram®, or similar, lug soles for both summer and winter boots (see a later section). However, you can obtain sufficient traction from summer boots with crepe (foam) soles when used on dry rock and soil, and they will do less environmental damage. They will slip on clay soils and wet leaves, and these soles do wear faster than lugged soles.

A proper fit is very important. Both boots that are too small and too large can result in severe blisters. Try the boots with the socks that you propose to wear in them. The accepted means of judging proper fit involves pushing the foot forward in an unlaced boot, and determining how much space there is behind the foot. One index finger should just fit. More fingers may mean the boots are too loose. If when you lace the boots you can bring the two sides together, then the boots are too small, or not built for your feet. I prefer a boot large enough that I can obtain a proper fit with an innersole in place. This gives me an opportunity to attach to the bottom of the inner sole the padding I need to correct the way my foot lines up (pronation and arch height). The inner sole provides both insulation and cushioning.

Boots that are too narrow can result in very painful feet. Boots that are too wide result in loss of proper foot support as the foot falls off center in the boot. Boots that have a rear portion that is too wide can be as much trouble as those in which the forward portion is too wide.

If you have foot problems, make sure you fit your boots with the proper foot supporting devices (orthotics). Also note that some knee and hip pain may result from the need for orthotics. Commonly, people over forty begin to need arch supports (a form of orthotic), because of falling arches. The amount of lift under the arch is critical, since too much lift can also cause misalignment and pain. You can make and adjust the amount of lift by applying one or more layers of patches of Dr. Scholl's® "Foot & Shoe Padding" or "Molefoam" to the underside of your innersoles. Again, if you are going to need innersoles or orthotics for your new boots, be sure the boots you buy have room for them.

I recommend Moleskin® for relief of sore spots due to boot rub. Adhesive tape may stick better in wet or cold conditions, but must be applied before the blister develops. Friends and I have used duct tape, either on the foot, or inside the boot, to prevent blisters. It sticks so well to feet, that you should not apply it over a blister.

The lightweight nylon (Cordura®) and leather boots offer an important option for summer hikers. They will not keep your feet dry in the rain. They breathe, and they will keep your feet happy, if you find:

1) A good fit,
2) Good ankle support, and
3) A substantial sole thick enough to cushion the foot from the very rough treadway.

See WINTER GEAR below for a discussion of winter boots. The possible conditions and weather govern your choice of boots in the spring and fall.

SWEATER: A sweater that opens in front gives more ventilation control. Down sweaters are light, and compress easily for carrying. However, they are a mess when soaked. Some people use the upper half of a quilted thermal suit. Wool, though relatively heavy, still seems best to some. Pile, though expensive, represents the state-of- the-art. Synthetic pile allows moisture to rapidly drain to the bottom of the sweater, where you can wring out the water. In cold weather you can brush off some of the moisture condensing, or forming frost, on the outside of the pile.

UNDERWEAR: Polypropylene and several similar fabrics have become the materials of choice in underwear and long underwear. These materials are available in several weights and styles. As mentioned above, avoid cotton.

RAINGEAR VERSUS WIND GEAR: Ideally, a garment worn as an outer layer (shell) should serve as both a waterproof and windproof item. Gore-Tex® is a material that is meant to be both breathable and water resistant. While many people buy garments made of this material at premium prices, look carefully at what the manufacturer guarantees. When you need a shell to stop the wind but allow controlled moisture transfer, an uncoated nylon parka or jacket would probably be the best solution. It must be big enough to allow you to wear any necessary insulating layers underneath. If you really want a garment that will keep the precipitation away from your clothing and body, then high quality, waterproof, coated fabric rain gear is probably the best bet. Uncoated nylon wind gear is so light that you could carry it in addition to raingear. I wear a Gore-Tex® parka in the winter, and carry a coated nylon rain jacket in the summer.

Below tree line I use an umbrella. You can wedge the handle between the pack frame and pack.

Generally, a silicone or fluorocarbon based compound is applied to fabric raingear. This makes the surface slippery. We do this to lower the surface tension, which keeps the water as drops that do not soak into the fabric. Put drops of water on your raingear. Do they soak in or do they remain as drops that could run off the garment? If the garment still retains some of the water repellent chemical, you may be able to renew its effectiveness by ironing the fabric (medium heat). I have found reference to only three products you could use to replace the repellent chemical. These are:

1) Scotchgard® by 3M, which you spray on,
2) Teltron®, another spray on product, and
3) Nikwax TX Direct®, which you wash into all layers of
   the fabric (undesirable for wicking layers).

PARKA: The term "parka" once referred to a hooded pullover used by the Eskimos. Nowadays the term also refers to jackets with hoods. Because of the greater flexibility in comfort control, the fully zippered, hooded jacket is preferred over a pullover, or a jacket without a hood. The term "parka" refers to both the down parka worn at stops in the winter, or in extreme weather, and to the uninsulated shell worn during most winter hiking. You can carry such a shell as windy weather gear in the summer.

In all cases, it is helpful to have a full front opening for a temporary increase in ventilation without having to remove the pack. Both types of parkas should have cuff adjustments or knit cuffs, bottom or waist closure (drawstring or Velcro®), pockets not covered by the waist band of your pack, and a hood deep enough that it can be drawn up to cover your forehead, cheeks and chin while you wear a hat. A hood this large can give you some protection from the bright sun in the spring. Since zippers may stick or ice up when you need them most, the parka should have snaps or Velcro® in addition to a zipper as a safety measure. Choose the material carefully. A parka should be breathable, and it should be long enough to cover your buttocks. You should carry a parka shell year round.

WIND PANTS: These should be lightweight, loose fitting, and should come well up on the torso (consider suspenders). They should not be airtight. There should be access to pockets in the inner pants. You can wear wind pants with long underwear and shorts (without pants) to provide good air circulation. You should reduce the bagginess of wind pants around the calf by wearing gaiters when wearing crampons. Do this in order to reduce the likelihood of your catching a crampon in the ballooned pant and then stabbing your calf or ankle. Wind pants should have separating zippers down the outside seams to make it possible to put them on without having to take off crampons, boots or snowshoes.

You should consider putting on wind pants whenever there is a need to conserve body heat. They account for an amazing difference in overall body warmth. Like other clothing items, they reduce the chance your feet will freeze. Some breathable nylon wind pants fold into a small enough package to fit into a parka pocket. I recommend that *rain* pants be carried in the summer.

PONCHO: Ponchos tend to blow over the head leaving the weather side exposed, but they provide adequate ventilation to minimize condensation. A foul weather suit is heavier, and, being a closer fit, results in more perspiration. A poncho is useful in emergency situations as a ground cloth, shelter, or would-be **cagoule** (loose, long, hooded garment best described as a wearable tent) or bivouac sack.

SCARF: Because it reduces necessary air circulation, many consider a scarf to be of negative value. To keep your neck warm, keep your parka hood up, or wear shirts or sweaters with high necks. A headband worn loosely around the neck is helpful. A balaclava will keep the neck warm as well as the head. Some wear neck warmers. You will probably want to remove whatever you have around your neck when you are working hard going uphill.

I discuss **HATS, MITTENS** (gloves), and **SOCKS** in the section on Winter Gear.

EQUIPMENT

PACK: While the packframe and sack combination is my choice for most summer and winter overnights, the beginner may want to consider a day pack for a first purchase.

There is a greater tendency to carry adequate equipment and clothing when space is available, as with a large packframe sack that has plenty of pockets. You can easily carry a pack that is not full, but it is difficult to tie on very much when the pack is too small. Hold-open stays are helpful with pack frame sacks. Top flaps should have quick release fittings on the hold down cords, workable with mittens on your hands. You should look for a sack made of waterproof material. Packframe waist straps help relieve the load on the shoulders. Chest (sternum) straps help too, though some find them uncomfortable. It is essential to select and adjust the correct size of frame to fit your torso. Internal frame packs have become popular, but I recommend that you try one on an extended trip before you choose this style over an external frame pack.

In my opinion fanny packs are not large enough to contain adequate clothing for mountain travel. Large fanny packs tend to carry the load lower than is comfortable for long hikes. The weight drops down onto the buttocks rather than remaining on the waist. It is possible to attach shoulder straps to a large fanny pack.

A small "fanny pack" worn in front of the body can provide an excellent place to keep your lunch, small water bottle, and map. You will not have to stop to get out a candy bar! You also have a convenient place to put the wrapper. Another advantage of a fanny pack worn on the front is that it partially balances the weight of the pack on the back.

SLEEPING BAG: Down has been the sleeping bag insulation of choice for backpackers (hikers who camp overnight). A summer bag should contain 1 to 2 pounds of down, while the winter bag should have at least 2 1/2 to 3 1/2 pounds of down or more. Look carefully for:

1) Tube construction without sewn through seams (there should be no stitching connecting the inside and outside shells except at the zipper and around the hood),
2) Down without feathers (if possible),
3) Fabric which is down-proof, ripstop and breathable, and
4) Differentially cut inner and outer shells (the outer shell should be bigger than the inner shell).

In the winter you should have a bag with a hood that you can draw up to cover everything but the nose. For winter use, consider some combination of inner and outer bags that you can use separately in the summer. In winter, the bag has to be large enough so that you can bring into it those items that you must keep warm or readily available, such as:

inner boots, water bottles, mittens, flashlight, hat, etc. On the other hand, a bag that is too big will keep the insulation too far from the body and allow convection currents.

Before you buy, try the bag out to see if you will fit. You may want the bag large enough so that you are able to draw your knees up inside the bag to dress. The bag should not be tight around the hips or shoulders.

You should air your sleeping bag during breakfast to reduce the accumulated moisture. In the mountains your sleeping bag is your last resort for warmth, and it is neither comfortable nor warm when wet.

You should not rely heavily on temperature ratings for sleeping bags. You can draw a better prediction of relative warmth from the loft (overall thickness when fluffed) of the bag. For below zero conditions, you need from seven to nine inches of loft, or more.

A winter sleeping bag will be much too warm when used in the summer, unless you can unzip it and place your feet outside. Full length zippers provide this capability, but they increase the weight of the bag, and they decrease the insulating properties.

On extended winter trips, sleeping bags soon accumulate a burden of body moisture and frost melt that can, in a matter of days, render the bag soggy. Sleeping bags made with synthetic insulation do not lose as much insulating value when wet, but are very bulky to pack.

PAD: Since it is illegal and environmentally destructive to cut boughs to use for a mattress, as was done when I was young, some sort of pad or mattress is essential. If you sleep cold, ask yourself if it is the bottom side of you that is the most cold. You compress the sleeping bag under you, and therefore it has very little insulating capability. The insulation provided by the pad determines how cold you will be. In the summer, you need at least $1/2$ inch of closed-cell foam to provide the necessary insulation. In the winter you will probably want twice as much insulation. If your pad is not full length, then you will need to have sufficient gear and clothing to put under your head, legs, and particularly your feet.

A recent innovation involves an air mattress filled with open-celled foam and marketed under the name "Therm-A-Rest®." Though somewhat heavier, these mattresses are more comfortable than closed-cell foam pads.

A closed-cell foam pad with transverse ridges has become popular. It is marketed under the name "RidgeRest®." It provides a set of dead air spaces and increased effective thickness with reduced weight.

FLASHLIGHT: A C-size, two cell flashlight with alkaline batteries and halogen bulb make a good combination for a flashlight. However, a headlamp frees the hands for climbing, rescue work, or just doing camp chores. Carry a spare bulb and spare batteries. With a two-cell flashlight, you can reverse a battery, when not in use, to prevent discharge. You can also accomplish this by inserting a piece of plastic next to one of the batteries in order to ensure an open circuit. Do not forget to reverse the battery or remove the plastic when you need light.

Ask about the cost of batteries and their expected life before you buy the light. Some of the lithium batteries for headlamps are very expensive, and some headlamps only take specially sized lithium batteries.

Batteries give more light, if you keep them warm. A headlamp with a remote battery holder worn inside clothing is the best solution for winter use.

Before each trip I use a digital voltmeter to check the voltage of the batteries in my headlamp or flashlight. Do not assume that new batteries are fully charged. A conventional carbon-zinc battery and an alkaline battery should have a voltage of about 1.55 volts when new and less than 1.3 volts when discharged. I do not take batteries to the mountains that have a voltage of less than 1.50 volts. You may have to determine from experience the corresponding voltages for the special battery needed for your headlamp. Some headlamps use 4.5 volt batteries made of three conventional batteries. The discharged voltage would be less than 3.9. The lithium battery for my headlamp has a voltage of 2.9 when new, and I have not had it long enough to give you a report on the discharged voltage.

Halogen bulbs give more light for the same battery drain, but cost a little more. Some discount stores carry these bulbs at reasonable prices.

STOVE: The brass, pint-size, white gas, self-pressurizing stove (Svea® 123) once was the most popular. In winter it would go out unless you insulated it from the snow. All gasoline stoves sold today have pumps, and are more dependable, but they have more parts to replace (or lose).

I recommend that you use the special fuel made for stoves and lanterns, because of its freedom from the penetrating odor characteristic of most white (unleaded) gasoline.

If your stove burns with a yellow flame, combustion may be incomplete. The stove may be producing carbon monoxide, as well as, a lot of black on the bottom of pans. Be safe. Ventilate the space in which you cook. Be safe. Fill your stove outside your tent. Butane and propane stoves are convenient, but are heavier for extended use. They will not burn at very low temperatures. Some people use Sterno® (a jelly-like fuel that comes in a can that is the burner), because of its dependability. It is free from the mechanical problems of stoves employing liquid fuels. Note that you do need a special stove (stand) in which to use the Sterno can.

A recent innovation is the solid fuel stove with a fan that will burn pieces of wood, cones, bark, etc. It does not require fossil fuel, but it does require batteries to run the fan. This could be a handy stove in a dry climate on an extended trip. The batteries would be a lot lighter than the fuel left at home. The stove probably will not be much help to anyone, even the very dedicated, when the conditions are very cold, ice covered and snowy.

FUEL CONTAINER: A gasoline fuel container has come to mean an aluminum bottle available in various sizes from 11 up to 33 fluid ounces. Most of the available stoves will burn an ounce of fuel in 5 to 7 minutes while boiling a pint of water in about 3 or 4 minutes. Starting at 32 degrees F it takes at least 1.8 times as much heat, fuel and time to bring water to a boil, if you begin with ice or snow instead of water. This is because of the considerable heat of fusion. You need at least $1/3$ pint of fuel per person per day, unless you will be melting snow or ice for water. In that case, you may need about $2/3$ pint per person per day. My estimates may be conservative for the kind of cooking you do. Experience will show how much fuel your cooking requires. Carry extra fuel in case of spills, leaks, the unexpected need to boil drinking water, emergencies including rescues, or unexpected company.

WINTER GEAR

BOOTS: You should try any foot gear cautiously at temperatures much below freezing. Having good boots that will keep your feet warm is important, because you cannot count on your socks staying dry. Nowadays, plastic double-boots have become the usual boot for serious outings. These have the advantages of being relatively lightweight, impervious to water, and substantially insulated. While they are relatively rigid (a benefit for cramponing), they also work well on snowshoes.

Single-boots might suffice down to 10 degrees F., if the rest of the body is warm. Note that temperatures in the snow might be much colder than the air temperature above. Below zero, overboots (see below) might do the job, if your boots are not well insulated. Double and triple leather boots tend to be heavy, and should be investigated thoroughly before you pay a lot of money for them. Military surplus, insulated rubber boots ("Mouse Boots") provide very good insulation against the cold, but they are bulky, may chafe the shins, and do not hold crampons well.

Hikers not interested in cramponing or technical climbing should consider rubber bottom, leather top boots with liners. Liners are made of felt or of synthetic foam. The felt liners can absorb a lot of moisture unless protected by a vapor barrier (vapor barrier socks or plastic bags over socks). Make sure the foam liners have closed-cell foam, or use vapor barrier liners. Snowmobile boots might also serve your needs.

No boot worn in the winter should be tight enough to restrict circulation or to squeeze the insulating thickness out of socks and boot liners. Removable innersoles of closed-cell foam provide critical insulation under the foot, and they will improve the warmth of any boot in which you can find room for them. Consider buying your winter boots sufficiently large to take an extra pair of innersoles.

Waterproofing of leather boots provides a vapor barrier on the outside, which helps account for why your socks become so wet. However, keeping out water is very important in winter. You could encounter water in streams and thaws.

SOCKS: Socks are available in pile, neoprene and knitted fabric. Pile socks are very comfortable, but their softness and stretchability may result in their sliding down to your toe. Neoprene socks I have seen are thick enough that you will need a larger boot to accommodate them. You may find them to be too tight with not enough give. Knitted socks come in cotton, wool blends, all wool, polypropylene, Gore Tex®, and blends with acrylic, nylon and cotton. Typical two layer systems for winter use involve an inner layer that is soft and medium thick, such as an athletic sock. The outer layer is thicker providing most of the cushioning and insulation. If you have room for a third layer, consider using a thin, wicking layer of polypropylene next to your skin. If you are using a vapor barrier in your boots, it should not be next to your skin.

Woven socks that are worn thin may only provide a mesh of thread between your skin and the innersole. If your feet are warm and moist, which results in their being soft, this mesh can irritate the skin. This irritation is particularly bad when the boots are sufficiently large that the foot moves back and forth in the boot with each step. Do not skimp on socks.

MITTENS: The biggest problem in keeping hands warm in cold weather is that of reducing the conduction away from them when objects, such as an ice axe and ski poles, are grasped firmly in use. A second problem is that of removing moisture from the mittens, caused both by snow melt and by insensible perspiration. I find that, if I put Snowseal® or other waterproofing on leather mittens, they seem clammy because of the trapped moisture. Similarly, I recommend that you not purchase shells made from waterproof material, since these will trap insensible perspiration and become damp rapidly. In very cold weather you may want to try some sort of palm liner in your mittens. I have used closely sheared sheepskin (hair must point towards the wrist or the liner will work out of the mitten), but a sheet of thin, closed-cell foam will work.

The usual set of layers on hands consists of glove liners (often polypropylene) under knitted woolen or synthetic pile mittens under mitten shells that have cuffs and are made of nylon cloth. You leave the glove liners on when you take your hands out of the mittens to perform intricate tasks. You can use knitted woolen or woven synthetic fingerless gloves for the same purpose as the glove liners, although you might not find these as warm.

Fingers stay warmer, if they can share their warmth. Outer gloves separate the fingers and surround them with heat draining material (the envelope is larger). The substantial material between fingers may squeeze the fingers, and reduce the blood circulation. For these reasons, you should not use outer gloves except for situations, or activities, in which your fingers are unlikely to be cold.

It is essential to have mittens on a retainer to prevent their sliding out of reach on steep slopes, particularly above tree line. Carry extra mittens in case one slides out of reach or the ones you are wearing become too wet.

Lightweight nylon shells are useful without liners at near freezing temperatures to keep the snow off your hands and they reduce windchill. When the lightweight shells are wet they require less heat energy from the hands to rewarm them than do woolen or pile mittens, after you have taken them off for some task.

GOGGLES: You can use goggles to reduce glare and wind blast, and to keep your eyes from freezing in really severe conditions. They should have dark lenses, side pieces to exclude glare from the side, and provision for good ventilation. When you warm up sufficiently to begin to give off moisture vapor from your skin, the moisture shows up first as condensation on the inside of the goggles. The tendency of goggles to fog is annoying. Make sure you do not direct your breath upward. Once fogged, you can clear your goggles by using your finger to wipe them or by wearing them part way up your nose, thereby increasing ventilation. Most ski goggles now available have a double lens that has a layer of air between the lenses. They are much more resistant to fogging. If you wear glasses, be sure to obtain a pair of goggles designed to fit over glasses.

FACE MASK: Before you buy a face mask try it on to make sure that all of your face is covered by it, your jacket hood, and your goggles. Make certain it does not have the tendency to slide down over your eyes (very annoying). The face mask must provide escape for respired moisture (your breath), or excessive goggle fogging will result. Knit hats that convert into face masks with one or more openings (if the hat has one opening, we call it a balaclava) are adequate for all but the worst conditions, and would make sense as summer gear. Suede face masks are lightweight, comfortable when damp, reasonably inexpensive, and slide less than fabric face masks.

Eyeglasses fog inside face masks! If you need glasses and cannot wear contact lenses, you will have to wear glasses without a full face mask. A lower face mask and goggles over the glasses will cover most of your exposed skin. Carefully evaluate whether or not all of your face is covered. When it is very cold you will find it difficult to keep your glasses from frosting up unless you wear goggles. When it is snowing you will find that snow will accumulate on the inside surface of your glasses, if it is concave. Try a billed cap over a balaclava. To keep glasses free of frost, do not breathe on them and do not perspire.

Whether your goggles have glass or plastic lenses, they might not block ultraviolet light that is harmful to your eyes in the long run. UV light is a cause of cataracts. This concern is particularly important for those who go above tree line on snow where the glare is intense. Check the labels of goggles for the rated UV protection, and compare brands.

Drop your goggles around your neck when not in use. If they are on top of your forehead, overhead branches might pluck them off your head.

HATS: When it is very cold, wear two layers on your head in addition to your hood. A lightweight, synthetic pile balaclava and a pile hat work well together. When it is even colder try a face mask as well, but look for one that completely covers the head and neck. If you rely on a hat to keep your ears from freezing, be careful to select one that really does cover all of your ears. In the 1997 Canadian Ski Marathon my hat covered all but one half of an inch of each ear, which became badly frozen. The second day I found that my light balaclava kept me sufficiently warm, and offered the opportunity to adjust the amount of coverage of my head and neck in response to whether or not I was going uphill. I also used my hood.

GAITERS: We call short gaiters, around six inches high, scree guards. Their function is to keep pebbles from entering the top of your boots. Winter gaiters are usually fourteen to eighteen inches high. Some are insulated. They should go on and off easily, keep snow out of the tops of your boots, prevent snow coming in around the bottom of the gaiters, and be somewhat loose around your ankle (if they are to provide air space insulation). Loose gaiters can best be constructed with zippers, but the zippers should be provided with a flap to reduce ice-up. Loose gaiters tend to slide down; you can counteract this by sewing a small piece of Velcro tape to the side of the pant leg and the matching part to the inside of the gaiter. Gaiters made of heavy (stiff) materials, such as Cordura®, stay up better.

Do not buy your gaiters until you have your winter boots; you want the gaiters big enough to go around those monster boots.

To keep the feet from sweating you may want to avoid wearing gaiters when the Windchill Temperature is higher than 10 degrees F., unless you are in loose snow where you need gaiters to keep the snow out of the boots.

Super Gaiters are half way between gaiters and overboots. They have a rubber band (called a rand) which fits tightly around the boots just above the sole. An adhesive holds it on the boot. The gaiters are permanently attached to the top of this band. Such a boot and gaiter combination is suitable for use only in cold weather.

A cord sewn into the bottom seam of cuffless pants and tied to boot laces could eliminate the need for gaiters, at least with high boots and moderate, non-technical conditions.

OVERBOOTS: While overboots are seldom used nowadays (Super Gaiters are used), they are something you could make to supplement what you have in the way of boots. These are loose fabric boots worn over leather climbing boots to provide additional warmth. The fabric soles do not provide traction, so you can only wear overboots with crampons that have strap bindings, or with snowshoes. They should go on and off easily, and keep snow out of the tops of boots. They should provide insulation under the boot, over the instep, and over the toes (the crampon straps compress the latter two areas). Put overboots on before your feet are numb. Some people wear them whenever they wear their crampons (you will not have to adjust the crampons fit). Some use large felt innersoles inside the overboots to reduce heat conduction from boots to crampons. If there is bare ground, overboots are not the solution to the inadequate boot problem.

Both gaiters and overboots might come to you constructed with waterproof, coated nylon. Because the waterproofing traps moisture in, consider it undesirable. You can remove this coating by sandpapering the coated side of the fabric in order to increase the transfer of water vapor away from the boot.

Caution, overboots reduce the solid contact between boots and crampons, particularly when you use insulation under the boot. Sometimes the crampons roll off the boot to one side after the straps loosen.

CRAMPONS: These are sets of 10 or 12 spikes (or more) on a framework that straps to the bottom of the boot. More often than not, you need crampons in the winter and early spring on peaks above tree line. Either the peak has a steep snow pack, or the snow has blown away. Subsequent rainstorms will have left ice. Often, the ice is two inches thick on everything. I recommend that beginners interested only in walking on relatively flat ice use ten-point crampons, if available. Twelve-point crampons, with the two additional points sticking out in front, enable a climber to ascend vertical ice. Twelve-point crampons, the kind available now, require more expertise. They represent more of a threat to the user, since the forward pointing spikes could damage the other ankle, or calf.

Crampons should fit the boot snugly. Most crampons sold today are adjustable; you can make them fit a wide variety of boot shapes and sizes. Whether or not you wear overboots, check crampon strap tension after you have worn the crampons for a while, and tighten, if necessary. The crampon points should be about one- and-a-half inches long, and they should be sharp. Dull crampons can slide on ice just when you do not wish to skate.

So called "step-in" bindings provide an opportunity to put crampons on quickly. This is important, since it is usually windy and cold at the time when you put crampons on your boots. You can only use step-in bindings with stiff boots and without overboots. They do offer a secure means of attachment.

Instep crampons with only four points (these are also called creepers), strap on under the arch of the foot. They may be helpful on horizontal ice, or icy snow, but are not a substitute for twelve-point crampons on ice with any significant slope.

IF CRAMPONS ARE NEEDED, THEN AN ICE AXE AND SELF-ARREST INSTRUCTION ARE ALSO NECESSARY.

ICE AXE: An ice axe is a combination pick and adze head on a shaft with a metal spike at the other end. You can use one for cutting steps in ice, arresting a fall, belaying a roped party, as a walking stick, and for gaining purchase on ice as in ice climbing. The usual length of an axe to be used primarily for hiking and high angle snow climbing is equal to the distance from the palm of the hand to the floor when the elbow is slightly bent. Currently most people buy a short ice axe (70 centimeters or less), since short ice axes are used for ice climbing. Many of these people will never ice climb. They may never know how useful that longer axe could have been for crossing streams or bracing in high winds.

You can prevent abrasion of the lower shaft by wrapping it with electrical tape or duct tape. You can wrap the head of the axe with adhesive tape to reduce the heat conduction from the hand to the metal.

I urge you to bring an ice axe whenever you will be on ice or steep snow above tree line, but you should also bring the knowledge of how to self-arrest. Proficiency in the use of the axe comes only after instruction and practice of proper technique. You need to be able to arrest with the axe in either hand. Proper technique is important as is the strength to keep the ice axe in the proper position. Climbers sometimes die after falling on their ice axes. Injury from ice axe puncture is most likely to occur when the climber is falling out of control or in an avalanche.

SKI POLES: Swinging the arms while poling increases the stride, builds shoulder muscles, relieves the legs of some of the work, and assists the hiker up steep slopes. Ski poles are more effective than an ice axe in soft snow, and you can use them to brace yourself to maintain your balance. When above timberline travel does not involve risk of sliding off the mountain, it makes sense to take only ski poles and not an ice axe. You can use ski poles to push down the toe of a snowshoe when extricating the tail. You can plant them in back of the snowshoe of the person in front of you on a steep slope to reduce the possibility of that person sliding back down toward you. However, they are a nuisance on a bush-whack through thick going. They can be hazardous to the person behind you when they slip and thrust backward on steep going. After using snowshoe (ski) poles all day for balance, you may find yourself unsteady without them.

Ski pole baskets should be about 4 to 6 inches in diameter. Larger baskets have a greater tendency to catch on branches and roots. Smaller baskets do not give enough support in soft snow

CANTEEN: Plastic canteens or water bottles have several advantages over metal types, including light weight and lower heat conductivity. Some hikers use a 500 milliliter (18 fluid ounce) plastic hip flask that they can carry in a pocket to provide better accessibility and to reduce the chance of freezing. Others carry this size canteen on a cord around their neck and inside several layers of clothing.

Liter size bottles come in both wide mouth and small mouth styles. It is harder to drink from a wide mouth bottle without spilling, but they are easier to break into when frozen, easier to fill, and easier to load with pieces of snow, or ice, to melt in warm weather. If just the top of your water bottle freezes, try turning it upside down for a few minutes. There may be enough warmth left in the remaining water to thaw the ice sufficiently to release the top. You can use socks to insulate water bottles, but insulated water bottle jackets are available for one-liter bottles.

You may encounter, as I have, mildew in your plastic canteen after many years of use. Wet the cap and clean the inside, upper surface carefully with a paper towel. You may be surprised by how much slime can accumulate there.

It helps to put warm water (say, 140 degrees F., not boiling) into the canteen in the morning in the winter. It will remain thawed longer. You will be more likely to drink as much as you should, if the water is not too cold. You must keep plastic water bottles away from flames, and boiling water is too hot for them. As the boiling water, and the air above it, cools and contracts in volume, the closed water bottle will collapse and possibly crack.

VACUUM BOTTLE: For extra comfort and safety, something hot to drink should be available on a winter trip. This is possible when you carry a vacuum bottle (thermos). When camping overnight, you can have a hot drink during the night and/or while breakfast is being prepared. You can refill the bottle after each meal. The hot drink saved all day for an emergency may provide a pleasant moment after the hike while the car is warming.

You can further reduce heat loss from a vacuum bottle by covering the bottle with a sock. Glass vacuum bottles with plastic shells stay warmer much longer than metal vacuum bottles with metal shells, but do not drop your bottle!

SNOWSHOES: See Chapter 10 under SNOWSHOEING

AVALANCHE TRANSCEIVER: In the West there are too many slopes covered with snow that cannot be evaluated daily by avalanche experts. People traveling where there is any possibility of an avalanche should each carry an avalanche transceiver. This device emits a radio signal continuously. Each unit also has the capability of being used as a receiver. The person on the surface, using the receiving mode, can quickly home in on the location of a buried transceiver by making passes first along and then across the slide path.

When considering what to take on a hike remember that you must strike a balance between having everything you could need and being able to travel faster. The lighter load means that you have less risk of hurting yourself and of becoming benighted. The heavier load should provide more protection from the extremes of weather.

How much can a person carry? Conventional wisdom says that you should not carry more than the equivalent of one third of your body weight on your back. In the winter you could find that you are also carrying another one sixth of your body weight in the way of clothes and equipment on your body and feet.

CLOTHING AND EQUIPMENT CHECKLISTS

WHAT TO BRING ON SUMMER DAY TRIPS

Clothing worn or carried
Hiking boots and socks
Shorts
Tee shirt or similar shirt
Warm shirt (wool or acrylic)
Long pants (not cotton)
Sweater
Rain gear including pants
Light windbreaker
Warm hat and mittens
Sunglasses

Equipment carried in your pack
Flashlight or headlamp
Spare batteries & bulb
Compass & Map
Guidebook
Pocket Knife
Toilet paper
First Aid kit
Boot laces
Spare eyeglasses
Matches/butane lighters
Camera, film, filters
Whistle
Plastic bag for clothes
Sunscreen & lip balm
Insect repellent

Food and Water
2 liters of water, or more
Lunch & snacks to share

Equipment carried by the group
Group First Aid kit
Group bivouac sack, fly or tent

ADDITIONAL CLOTHING AND EQUIPMENT TO BRING FOR FALL, WINTER, AND SPRING DAY TRIPS

Clothing worn at the start
Long underwear
Pants: wool or synthetic
Shirt and/or second layer of
    polypropylene
Pile pullover
Boots and socks
Mittens, liners, and shells
Gaiters
Hat
Parka

Personal Equipment
Ski poles or ice axe
Crampons
Snowshoes w/creepers

Clothing carried in reserve
Wind pants
Down or heavy pile parka
Shirt or light sweater
Face mask
Balaclava
Extra mittens
Dry socks
Goggles

Additional group gear
Sleeping bag
Tent or bivouac sack
Stove and kettle
Foam pad (mattress)
Thermos bottle

ADDITIONAL CLOTHING AND EQUIPMENT TO BRING FOR OVERNIGHT TRIPS

Personal sleeping bag
Foam pad(s)
Candle lantern & candles
More dry socks
Down bootees (winter)
Tent & ground sheet (poly)
Tooth care supplies

Cook stove w/screen
Fuel bottle(s)
Stove base (for use on snow)
Cook kit
Spoon, cup & bowl
Cup for measuring, and
    scooping snow

OTHER ITEMS YOU MIGHT WANT

Plastic bag for collecting snow
Vapor Barrier sleeping bag liner
Vapor barrier socks or plastic bags
Water purifying pills or pump w/filter
Thermometer & wind meter
Spare matches or lighters

Fanny pack for lunch
Umbrella
Additional nylon cord
Plastic bag for garbage
Hat with visor
Journal & pencil/pen

continued on next page

Shovel for snow shelters & rescue
Mitten cord (retainer)
Bow saw or light axe
More toilet paper
Waterproof pack cover

Avalanche transceiver
Large water jug
Alarm clock
Repair kit
Pill kit

The repair kit and pill kit I carry deserve some comment. The repair kit contains such things as needles, yarn and thread, baling wire, a small pair of pliers, parts for the stove, spare screws and an Allen wrench for my crampons, a dime and a quarter, split rings, a spare pin for my pack, small scissors, a razor blade, and diaper pins. My pill kit includes small quantities of aspirin, ibuprofen, vitamin C, Benadryl®, quinine sulfate, a few Band Aids®, and a small container of Bag Balm®. On long trips it includes a daily vitamin supplement. Your kits should include those items you have found you need or might need.

ITEMS CARRIED IN THE CAR

Change of clothes with a sweater
Vacuum bottle of hot drink (winter day trips) or large water bottle
A snack with enough to share with others
(Winter) Snow shovel, chains, jumper cables, windshield scraper, and
    snow brush

THINGS TO CHECK TWO NIGHTS BEFORE THE HIKE
(Save the last night for packing and rest. Some items you may find you are missing cannot be purchased late at night or early in the morning.)

- Do you have a retainer strap for your eyeglasses (You might not be able to recover eyeglasses dropped in a brook or lost in soft snow.)?
- Does your flashlight or headlamp work?
- Do you have fresh batteries for the camera, headlamp, and avalanche transceiver? Battery voltages?
- Does your car have enough gas for the early morning drive?
- Are you going someplace where a pre-plotted compass bearing might help?
- Is the stove full of fuel and working?

- Are your toenails in need of trimming?
- Are your crampons and ice axe sharp?
- Are there sufficient holes in your crampon and snowshoe harness straps?
- Are snowshoe harnesses thawed and adjusted from the previous trip?
- Do your snowshoes need varnish?
- Do any of your clothing items need mending?
- Do your boots or other equipment need waterproofing?
- Are there questions you need to ask the leader? (He or she might not be at home the night before the trip.)
- Is everything located, clean and ready?
- Have you checked the weather?
- Did you remember to obtain permission from landowners or park authorities?
- Have you bought all the items on your menu?

Well, that is quite a long list of things to take and check. I compare it to Grampa's query, "Got the toilet paper and matches?" Note that what you carry in your head is more important than the equipment you have with you. No matter how much or how little you carry in your pack you still must evaluate whether or not you have sufficient gear, energy, and time for the specific conditions at hand and those likely to occur during the remainder of the trip. ❋

FOOD AND WATER

FOOD AND ENERGY

Food is the source of energy, including heat energy, for the body. The energy value of food is expressed in Calories, however you can turn some foods into energy more quickly than others. When you are hiking and carrying a heavy pack you may be burning as many as five thousand Calories per day, which is a lot more than you burn watching TV! So do not skimp on Calories in your food, particularly at breakfast time. Appalachian Trail hikers find that they lose weight in spite of an insatiable appetite. Many of the high-Calorie foods you have to avoid at home are just what you need on the trail. Do not try to diet when hiking in the mountains. And there is no reason to take anything you do not like on a hike of modest length. You can take anything you relish, and you can justify it by arguing that it has importance in keeping your blood sugar up in order for you to stay alert and make good decisions.

You do need to consider the perishability of the foods you take to the mountains. One hot afternoon is long enough to ruin some foods that you would normally keep in the refrigerator. Some of the specialty cheeses are wrapped in a foil that eliminates the need for refrigeration until you open them. Read the labels carefully. Some of the hard salamis do not require refrigeration. Dry milk keeps well and is much lighter than whole milk. You can substitute jerky for fresh meat. Freeze-dried food keeps in warm conditions. Sailors bake their bread a second time to enhance its keeping quality. Hardtack keeps as long as you store it in a dry environment. Beans, rice, pasta, nuts, and grain keep well, if kept dry.

If you want to avoid dying on the mountain, then it is important to avoid becoming sick, which is perhaps the first step in dying. When it comes to avoiding sickness there are some precautions you can take in choosing foods to eat. Canned food that is not properly prepared could contain any of many poisonous agents. Botulism is a severe form of poisoning of this type, and it can result in fatal paralysis. Beware of canned foods (including some foods in bottles) in containers that have seals that are broken, or even dents in the can. If the interior of the can is rusted or corroded, throw it away. If the bottle is vacuum sealed, the center of the lid should be depressed (concave). You should hear a "whoosh" when you open the bottle.

Natural degradation can transform oils and grease in food to less digestible forms of oil. This process makes food rancid, and there is a characteristic odor. The degradation progresses faster in warm conditions; use refrigeration to slow the process. Some foods stored at room temperature, might be rancid when you are ready to use them. Flour is a food that we do not associate with oils, but whole wheat flour contains enough oil so that it, too, can become rancid. If you eat rancid foods, you are likely to experience heartburn, flatulence, and indigestion.

Raisins, prunes and dried apricots are commonly treated with sulfur dioxide to prevent degradation by bacteria and maggots. Other dried fruits might also be so treated. The sulfur dioxide, or its byproducts, apparently can also kill helpful bacteria in the stomach. The result is indigestion. If you do not eat raisins at home but do eat them every day on the trail, then they might be a cause of your indigestion or diarrhea in the mountains. You may want to find other items to put in your **GORP** (good old raisins and peanuts), or you could buy unsulfured, dried fruit at an organic food store.

At home you are unlikely to suffer from malnutrition, if you eat a balanced diet. On the trail you are likely to eat foods that have been dried or otherwise processed. They will have lost some of their vitamins. If your trip is to be more than a week long, you should think about how you will ensure that you receive a balanced diet with inclusion of the necessary vitamins. For instance, it only takes a few weeks for scurvy to begin to make inroads on your body, if your diet is deficient in antiscorbutics like vitamin C, found in raw fruits and vegetables.

MENU RECOMMENDATIONS

The assumption made in the following recommendations is that light weight is better, because you will have to carry the food.   I also assume that you can obtain water at the point of food preparation, at least by melting snow. Clearly, the weight of fuel required to melt snow is far less than the weight of water obtained. However, in some circumstances providing a fire for melting snow is not feasible or time does not allow it. Then you must carry water, unless a stream provides a dependable source. See a later section regarding the safety of water in the outdoors.

In many tales of expeditions one person bought all the food, and the other members found to their dismay that they had to eat a repetitious menu of items that only the purchaser found appealing. The menu was both boring and unappetizing. Everyone in the expedition should make a review of the menu before you make purchases. During the short, two-person expeditions I have been on we have alternated who provides and prepares dinner (Note that he or she who cooks first carries lighter loads on the following days. If there is an odd number of suppers, he or she carrying the greater number cooks first.). Individuals provide lunches and breakfasts for themselves. On canoe trips (usually three canoes) we have also taken turns providing the dinners. This adds variety and challenges the providers to do their best.

If you were to think like a nutritionist, then you would look carefully at food choices. For instance, among the dried fruits, apricots and bananas are said to provide lots of potassium. Among the nuts, almonds have lots of potassium and a better balance of proteins than other nuts. If you do not like powdered milk, do you get enough calcium? For a more extensive discussion, see *The Athlete's Kitchen* by Nancy Clark.

BREAKFAST: The typical breakfast on the trail involves instant oatmeal. Even with the sugar and flavoring in the typical package the resulting gruel is none too appetizing. I repackage two commercial packets along with powdered milk, wheat germ, nuts and raisins. In the winter I have added cheese or butter after the hot water. Unfortunately the cheese and butter, being frozen, soak up a lot of heat, and cool the oatmeal substantially.

The oatmeal mix is not fully satisfying, so I also eat a bagel or English muffin (while the water is heating). You could substitute other hot cereals for oatmeal. The problem with cereals that are not instant is that you must cook them, thereby soiling a pot and adding 20 to 30 minutes to the time it takes to get ready for the trail.

Consider preparing bannock, which is a baking powder biscuit you "bake" in a frying pan or using a Bake-Packer® (See "Baking" later). You can incorporate raisins, cinnamon, cheese or meat.

During most of my adventures there has been a need to make an early start. As a result it has become important to expedite the preparation of breakfast. I limit breakfast to those items that I can eat cold or prepare by adding hot water. You can substitute granola (high in Calories; eaten cold) for oatmeal. You can use a GORP mix instead (See Snacks). Breadstuff can serve, such as, date nut bread, biscuits, fruitcake, cold toaster pastries, cereal bars, pancakes brought from home, and sweet rolls.

If you are only lukewarm in your feelings about granola as a breakfast food, I recommend that you try Marsha Westerberg's version of Mary Hunt's recipe for:

GRAINOLA

Mix the following ingredients, spread in two cookie sheets, and bake for one hour at 200 degree, stirring once:

6 cups Oatmeal (one 18 oz. box)

2 1/4 cups Wheat Germ

1 1/2 tsp. Vanilla extract

3/8 cup Cooking oil or olive oil

1/2 cup Honey

Add when cool:

1 1/8 cups Raisins

3/4 cup Sunflower seeds

1 1/8 cups Chopped walnuts or other nuts.

Mix thoroughly, and store in the refrigerator. None of these quantities is critical, but those above are for a mix we enjoyed this past summer. If you like your granola less sweet, then cut the volume of honey. If you eat your granola as a snack, you might want to add chopped dried fruit and different nuts.

Suggestions for drinks include tea, hot Tang, hot Jell-O, hot instant cider, hot chocolate (regular, fat free, or sugar free), coffee bags, instant coffee, and reconstituted powdered milk.

LUNCH: In the summer, days are long enough and the environment friendly enough so that you can prepare a meal when you stop, unless you are in the middle of a technical climb. Sandwiches seem to be the most common lunch, with a piece of fruit and a candy bar or other dessert. However, sloppy sandwiches do not travel well. Variations in sandwiches involve open faced "sandwiches" employing hardtack or similar bread, halves of bagels, or pocket bread. Peanut butter is a good source of Calories and some protein.

Think about the lunch contents you have envied (drooled over) when you have been out with others. Cheese, boiled eggs, carrot sticks, containers of flavored yogurt (if you freeze these ahead of time and insulate them, in the summer they will have the consistency of soft ice cream by lunch time), hard salami, dried apricots, containers of tabouli — all look good on the trail.

Fresh fruit is questionable in the wintertime since you must keep it from freezing. Oranges represent a particular problem, since you need to take your mittens off to peel them. In peeling oranges, you are likely to get juice on your fingers, making the fingers more prone to chill.

In cold conditions, frozen sandwiches are unappealing. You can carry them inside clothing to keep them thawed. On a multi-day trip you need something that you can eat frozen. Here is a recipe for a hard biscuit that is easily eaten when frozen, travels well, contains much of what you might like for lunch, and is easily made.

RECIPE FOR ETRUSCAN RUSKS (Courtesy of Laura Waterman)
  1 cup White flour
  1 cup Whole wheat flour
  1/2 cup Wheat Germ
  1/2 cup Powdered milk
  1/2 cup Melted butter or margarine (1 stick)
  1/2 cup Maple syrup.
Mix the dry ingredients, stir in the butter and syrup, and knead until you can shape the batter into cookies. You may have to add a little water, if the dough is too crumbly. Make a dozen round cookies of uniform thickness (about one half inch thick or less), and place on a cookie sheet. Bake for 10 to 15 minutes at 350 degrees until they just begin to turn brown. Longer cooking will make the rusks hard. Variations include addition of raisins or nuts and the substitution of oatmeal for wheat germ.

Two or three rusks can form the core of your lunch. You will find that they are heavy when you begin to make lunches for a multi-day trip, but you need that much food. I store any extra rusks in the freezer between hiking trips. Supposedly, these rusks are what the Roman soldiers ate. I will bet they used honey instead of maple syrup.

Lunch drinks could include canned V-8 juice, soda in cans, fruit juice (apricot nectar is my favorite) carried in plastic bottles, electrolyte replacement (such as Gatorade®), instant iced tea, and hot tea, Jell-O or Tang® in a thermos.

Note that when you place drinks other than plain water in a polyethylene "water" bottle, the organic matter in that drink, if not thoroughly cleaned out, can lead to a mildew that can be very persistent. For this reason, you may want to consider placing such drinks in liter size, reused soda bottles made of polyethylene terphthalate (recycle category 1) that have a harder, smoother surface. Because they are quite clear, you can see whether or not they are clean.

SUPPER: Be civilized. First prepare hot water for drinks and instant soup. A few crackers enhance the soup. You could serve cheese as well.

There are many delicious freeze-dried meals available. I find that I need a two-serving's size package of most brands to satisfy me when I am doing serious hiking. Instant (just add hot water) meal components are available in supermarkets. For instance, you can find an instant chili dish that has everything but the beans. You can find "instant" dried beans in your food co-op. Fantastic Foods sells them and you might find them in the Mexican food's section.

You can build suppers around a source of starch. I use:
1) Couscous (be sure to get the variety to which you need only add hot water),
2) Rice (I prefer 20 minute white rice to Minute Rice®; note that brown rice and wild rice need about 40 minutes of cooking time),
3) Pasta (there are so many choices, however, the thinner pastas cook quicker),
4) Dried tabouli (with or without flavoring; a little margarine improves this mix),
5) Bulgur (there are several spellings),
6) Turkey stuffing (contains lots of spices), or
7) Instant potatos.

I have used groats (barley), cracked wheat, and other grains, but they usually take longer to cook. You can find other possibilities in your food co-op. You can use the instant beans mentioned above as the base for a meal.

To any of the starch bases can be added a source of protein, such as a can of turkey, chicken, shrimp, tuna, corned beef, Spam® or sausages. Jerky and salami are other possibilities. It is legitimate to add or substitute nuts. Shaved almonds or pine nuts make a nice touch. They are lighter than canned meats. You may want to add butter (or margarine) or cheese. Then add a package of fresh, frozen, or freeze-dried peas or carrots. You could use sun-dried tomatos instead of the peas or carrots, particularly with pasta. If you dry your own vegetables, there are more choices. Finally, there is the matter of spices. I have used curry and cumin (both from the spice can and as a packaged sauce), marjoram on fish, thyme and rosemary on chicken, garlic on pasta, onion powder and dried mushrooms on beef or jerky, and do not forget the pepper. You should also consider taking fresh, or home dried, herbs since they weigh very little. If you prepare the carbohydrate base without meat, you could construct spicy sauces from soy, taco, spaghetti, or hot sauce. Dried soups with a little water will make a sauce, but there is a wide variety of packages of pasta-and-sauce already on the market.

For dessert there are many interesting possibilities. Try to save something for dessert that you have not had during the day. Examples include fruit cake, brownies, cookies, pound cake, freeze-dried ice cream (it is not quite what you expect, but definitely sweet), home dried apple sauce, Jell-O, mint patties, and instant pudding. In winter I have baked gingerbread using a BakePacker®, (see below) and added whipped topping (quite light to carry). Some people like fruit cocktail. The cans are heavy, and the dehydrated form takes quite a long time to rehydrate.

Suggestions for drinks include tea, instant coffee, Tang®, hot Jell-O, instant hot cider, more instant soup and hot chocolate. If you would like to try some other flavors, here is what I have tried. Mix two level tablespoons of dry milk and one tablespoon of instant pudding mix with eight ounces of water. Flavors available include vanilla, coconut cream, chocolate, pistachio and butterscotch. If you find you want more flavor, or a sweeter drink, use a heaping tablespoon of pudding mix. Sometimes the pudding mix does not dissolve well. You could start with the pudding mix and a little hot water. Once the mix is dissolved, add cold water and the powdered milk.

SNACKS: There seems to be an endless list of possibilities for a GORP mix. It is certainly possible to make GORP without raisins or peanuts. Ingredients that I have found particularly satisfying are dried pineapple slices chopped into small pieces, almonds with a tamari coating, jelly beans (very hard when cold; avoid the inexpensive varieties with all artificial flavors), freeze-dried cranberries, M&M's®, pretzel pieces, etc. Your food co-op will have bin after bin of possibilities.

You may find as I have that cheese is very welcome as a snack. Hard salami, particularly because it is salty, is also quite welcome. Beer nuts combine sugar, salt and fat; they can provide a change from your normal GORP or be included in it.

Granola bars have become a common snack item and source of energy. Perhaps you would like to make your own using the following recipe:

GRANOLA BARS (Courtesy of the Hulbert Outdoor Center)
  1 1/8 lb. Rolled oats
  2 1/2 cups Chopped nuts
  3/4 pound Brown sugar
  1/3 pound Peanut butter
  1/4 pound Melted butter
  3/4 cup Maple syrup
  1 1/2 tsp. Vanilla extract
  1 1/2 tsp. Salt
  1 1/2 cups Raisins, dried fruit, dates, apples.
               If you use fresh apples, limit these to not more
               than one half cup. They add a lot of moisture.
  1 1/2 cups Chocolate chips (optional)
Mix ingredients and spread in a 9 x 13 inch pan. If you like coconut, sprinkle some on top. Bake at 450 degrees for 10 to 12 minutes. The result may look raw and soft. Cool in the pan before cutting. Place in plastic bags or wrap in waxed paper. Store in the refrigerator.

The suggestions provided here do not begin to enumerate all the possible foods suitable for backpacking. I recommend that you try to bring variety to your menu. Sources of menu ideas include the Sierra Club's *Simple Foods for the Pack*, *The Athlete's Kitchen* by Clark, mentioned above, and *The One Pan Gourmet* by Jacobson. Whatever your menu choices, avoid trying anything new on the trail. There is plenty of opportunity to experiment with new food selections at home. You can also master camp cooking equipment at home on the kitchen stove or in the back yard.

Recently, I bought an electric food drier, and I have enjoyed my own dried carrots, beef, mushrooms, apple sauce fruit leather, cantaloup, and bananas. It certainly has lightened the food that I carry on the trail. By my next hiking season I hope to try dried broccoli, peaches, apples, and raspberries, among other foods. Home drying of foods provides an opportunity to save money, cut your pack weight, and try unusual dried foods. See *The Hungry Hiker's Book Of Good Cooking* by McHugh, *The Lightweight Gourmet: Drying And Cooking Food For The Outdoor Life* by Kesselheim, and *Making And Using Dried Foods* by Hobson.

CAMP COOKING TECHNIQUES

The several methods of camp cooking are heating, boiling, frying, broiling and baking with some variations.

Soaking, such as in reconstituting dried food, is another method of food preparation. It does not necessarily involve cooking. Reconstitution is slow for some foods, and you should not expect that boiling for twenty minutes will accomplish the same results as an overnight soak. Plan ahead. Note that a long rehydration is difficult to accomplish, if the air temperature is substantially below freezing. You could accomplish rehydration using a wide mouth bottle placed in the sleeping bag, or you could put the food being reconstituted in water and carry it all day. Warm water will speed the process somewhat, but hot water may change the texture of the food by prematurely cooking it.

BOILING: Heating and boiling are variations on the same theme. Both employ a pot over a fire. In heating a food, a boil may not be required. Some cook kits have nesting pots, which you can use as a double boiler. You keep the larger pot clean for heating water. Meals usually become one or two pot style, unless there is time for sequential cooking and cleaning.

Because of reduced atmospheric pressure, boiling is too easy at altitude; it occurs at lower and lower temperatures with increasing altitude. The time required to cook something becomes correspondingly longer and longer.

Table 12-1 - Boiling Temperatures at Altitude

Altitude		Adj. Std. Press.*		Boiling Temp.		Cooking Time
Km	Feet	mm Hg	psi	°C	°F	Increase (Approx.)
0	0	760	14.7	100.0	212	0%
1	3281	675	13.1	96.7	206	6%
2	6562	598	11.6	93.4	200	20%
3	9842	529	10.2	90.1	194	40%
4	13,123	467	9.0	86.9	188	
5	16,404	411	8.0	83.6	182	
6	19,685	360	7.0	80.3	177	
7	22,966	315	6.1	77.0	171	
8	26,247	274	5.3	73.7	165	

*The Adjusted Standard Pressure is the atmospheric pressure you would find at the specified altitude if the pressure at sea level was Standard Pressure (760 mm of mercury (Hg) or 14.7 pounds per square inch).

In fact, some foods do not cook adequately at temperatures much below 200 degrees (F), no matter how long you cook them. You can overcome this by means of a pressure cooker. Since pressure cookers are relatively heavy, in backpackers' terms, one usually uses them only at base camps. Note, that pressure cookers build a pressure above atmospheric pressure, which accounts for a higher boiling temperature and shorter cooking time. However, the pressure cooker can only handle one specific pressure differential (usually 15 pounds per square inch). If the atmospheric pressure is quite low, the pressure cooker might only achieve conditions similar to what they would be at sea level. In other words, the pressure cooker might not substantially shorten the normal cooking time when used at very high altitude, but that is much better than not cooking the food at all.

A variation on boiling is the boil bag. You place the food and an appropriate amount of water in a plastic bag that you then place in a pot with some water. The food in the plastic bag is cooked by the heat that goes through the plastic from the surrounding boiling water. The advantages of boil bags are that they do not soil the pot, and you can prepackage the dry meal in the boil bag. Some commercial, freeze-dried meals are so packaged. The disadvantage is that you end up with a bag that you must clean for reuse, or that you must carry out soiled. Another disadvantage is that the boil bag does not fill the pot. For a given volume of food you need a slightly larger pot when you use a boil bag. Use substantial plastic bags; you do not want your precious supper mixed in with all the boil water. I recommend that you use Glad® brand one gallon zipper closure bags. Do not seal them tightly. If tight, the steam created in the bag may lead to unacceptable expansion. Even if the expansion is slow, it will push the top off the pot, and there will be too much cooling of the top of the bag. Arrange the plastic bag so that the boiling water in the pot will not dilute the contents of the bag. The plastic bag with the top folded over, but not fully zipped, should do the job.

FRYING: Frying involves nothing difficult except for temperature regulation. Some camping stoves do not throttle down well. If the fuel is pressurized, try keeping the pressure low. The best results require practice and constant attention. Placing some water in the pan while it is still hot will aid in cleaning of the fry pan. Certainly heat aids the process of removing fat from the pan when using detergents.

Cooks differ in their philosophy as to how grease-free a clean pan should be. I believe that you should remove all the fat after use to avoid the stomach distress from rancid fat in a greasy pan.

BROILING: You can broil on a backpacking grill, or on one of woven green shrub stems. Choose your shrubs carefully, for some may contribute inedible juices or unacceptable flavor. Young birch trees have a very sweet taste like wintergreen. I recommend them.

In Nova Scotia I saw a chef broil a salmon by tying it to a plank set vertically next to a wood fire. The chef had to baste the fish often to keep it from drying. A metal trough collected the drippings. The flavoring of the basting liquid has a lot to do with the ultimate result, as does the species of hardwood burned in the fire. Though I have not tried them, hickory, maple and birch seem like woods that would result in suitable flavors. In regions where flat rocks (usually sedimentary) are available, you might use these in place of the plank. Do not forget to bring some expendable line for tying the steak or fish to the slab, and be prepared for the possibility that the stone might break from uneven thermal expansion. It is not Pyrex. I do not recommend this method of cooking for use in bear country.

BAKING: You can bake with a reflector oven. As a Boy Scout, I had unsatisfactory encounters with this device. Later, my brother taught me to maintain a small, hot fire with the oven quite close to the fire. Rotate the pan several times to ensure that you have cooked all sides evenly. It amazed me how good fresh pizza tasted in the wilderness on the Albany River in Ontario.

Another method of baking employs a device called a "BakePacker®." This is a grid of vertical aluminum plates about an inch high which sits on the bottom of the pot. You add water up to the top of the grid, and then place the dough in a one gallon boil bag (Glad® brand zippered bags are recommended) on top of the grid. The top of the bag is folded over but not zipped, and a cover is added. Using a medium boil for the usual baking time could yield such delights as corn bread, muffins, bannock, soda bread, ginger bread, biscuit, baked fish and omelets. Unfortunately the baked good takes on the shape of the interior of the bag, and the bag is a mess that you must carry off the mountain. Also, you may have difficulty retrieving the baked good without it crumbling. Still, the results are very tasty and especially appreciated in the outdoors. You can achieve similar results with a collection of stones about three quarters of an inch in diameter placed in the bottom of the pot and covered with water. In the winter such stones may not be available.

A third possibility for baking is with a homemade oven constructed from a three pound coffee can as described by Jacobson in his book *The One-Pot Gourmet: Fresh Food On The Trail.*

DISHWATER DISPOSAL: Dishwater disposal is a concern, because the dishwater might attract wild animals or the dog from the neighboring campsite. If you use only water and a spoon to clean the dishes, you can drink the dishwater. In the wintertime this is particularly appropriate, since any warm water is hard won. In the summer any grease left on the dishes or pots could become rancid. You should wash the dishes with soap or detergent after employing the spoon technique. Be judicious about where you dump dishwater. It may still attract animals. Dispose of it some distance from your tent and cooking site, but not close to a stream or other surface water.

WATER

The beginner is likely to encounter two simple reasons for lack of energy on a long climb, other than conditioning: hunger and thirst. In the summer, when there may be plenty to drink, sometimes hunger is hidden by liquid intake. In winter, you may know you are thirsty but not realize how dehydrated you are. Anticipating a trail without water, you should fill up beforehand. Take an extra water bottle with you on the drive to the trailhead. You may be surprised at how much you can drink, even after having several cups of liquid with breakfast. With this in mind, do not skimp on the amount of water you carry when you start hiking after an overnight camp.

It is important to note that dehydration can contribute to fatigue, hypothermia, heat prostration, heat stroke, dizziness, leg cramps, headaches, and a general feeling of malaise. If you allow your body to dehydrate, the blood becomes thicker (more viscous) and does not flow as easily. When the blood is thick, heat and energy providing glycogen are not distributed to the muscles where needed. In cold weather hypothermia can result. In hot weather the thicker blood does not do an efficient job of carrying waste heat to the skin, and hyperthermia might result.

You should be drinking two or more quarts of water during a strenuous hiking day, and much more in hot weather. You should be drinking at least another quart when you camp for the night. Athletes have found that it is much easier to consume adequate water that is lukewarm than it is to take in that much volume of cold or hot drinks. Have your hot drinks, but be sure the total intake is adequate.

Where does one find suitable drinking water? Suspect any water from surface streams. It could contain bacteria, viruses, protozoa and parasites. It could be a source of hepatitis or giardiasis. Use disinfectants. For those who use iodine pills, there is now a second treatment that can remove the undesirable iodine (taste) after it has had a chance to disinfect. Hypochlorite bleach (5% sodium hypochlorite) at a dose of one or two drops per gallon will be effective; it takes an hour or more to act. If you can just barely taste it, the dose is adequate. You are more likely to taste the chlorine when the water is tepid. The colder the water, the longer you should wait for the disinfectant to act.

Bringing water up to a temperature of 160 degrees F. will kill giardia (the organism which causes giardiasis, a parasitic disease of the intestinal tract), but it will take a long boil to kill resistant viruses.

Most pump operated water filters have not had filter openings small enough to remove viruses. However, some filter manufacturers now claim that their filters have small enough openings. You cannot expect a filter to begin to remove viruses unless the filter pore size is one half a micron or less.

In the wintertime, with a snow cover and no recent rainfall, streams will have receded to what we call "base flow," which comes from water stored in the ground. This water is more likely to be free of pollutants than would be surface water from recent rainfall. There could have been moose wading upstream. The surface water least likely to be polluted is that from a spring, provided there are no significant sources of pollution uphill, such as a privy.

In the wintertime, melting snow over a stove is the most dependable source of water, assuming there is snow on the ground. Below timberline the snow might be full of spruce and fir needles, bits of bark, and other debris. Above timberline there is usually a lot of wind blown inorganic (rock and soil) debris in the snow. Bring along an old handkerchief or piece of tee shirt to use as a filter. However, you will have more water quicker, and with less use of fuel, if you can find a source of running, or unfrozen, water. The advantage of using water as opposed to snow is that you do not have to provide the significant heat needed to melt the snow (heat of fusion). See the section on Fuel Bottles in Chapter 11 for a discussion of how much fuel you need. Spring water is usually slightly warmer than 32 degrees F and free of spruce needles. But springs can be covered by heavy snows and ice accumulations. You may need an ice axe.

Is a healthy, properly fed person likely to make better decisions than the same person when run down and ill? Again I emphasize that you need to eat and drink enough to match the amount of water you lose and food you burn during the hiking day. You do this in order to stay prepared to make those good decisions. The back cover shows me setting an example. ❄

SOME MOUNTAINEERING ETHICS

Ethics are disciplines, frameworks of ideas, or systems of values that define your moral position and from which rules are developed that apply to real life situations. Philosophers search for general, universal ethics such as the Golden Rule (do unto others as you would have them do unto you). However, the Golden Rule, applied alone, could be used to justify exploitation of the natural environment (I want mine, he can take his). A practical approach is to adopt applied ethics (rules), without answering the question of the underlying basis for morality. On the other hand, I suggest that enlightened self-interest means to you, the mountain hiker, that it is good to protect the environment for your future use, and that it is good (in your interest) to treat other people (and cultures) in the wilderness with respect, helpfulness and consideration. Based on these two ethical principles you can make a list of rules (applied ethics), such as: It is undesirable (except in emergencies) to make loud noise in the wilderness (mountains).

In my definition of good judgment (Chapter 1) I used the word "responsible." To be responsible is to make decisions, and take actions, consistent with ethics. The ethics (or rules) are relevant if you have adopted them, or if they will be used by others to judge your actions and these ethics are ones you respect. In the first case you are responsible to yourself, in the second case to others.

The purpose of this chapter is to acquaint you with a few of the ethical issues related to mountain hiking.

SEARCH AND RESCUE

A RESCUE ETHIC: Many climbing parties go into the mountains prepared to perform self-rescue, that is, to do whatever it takes to get the party "out of the woods" in the event of an injury or lost trail. In the winter self-rescue may be necessary to staying alive. Consistent with the view that the hiking party should get itself out is the acceptance of responsibility for reimbursement of any costs incurred by rescuers. If you believe in that responsibility, you are likely to make a greater effort to avoid accidents and to get the party out of the mountains. You would want to avoid both incurred costs and the unfortunate notoriety accompanying a rescue.

Rescuers often are asked to endure stormy conditions, sometimes at night, to reach an injured hiker or climber. They put their lives at risk. I bring to your attention that Albert Dow died in an avalanche on Mt. Washington (NH) while searching for two men lost in a winter storm. The risks the rescuers take can be substantially greater than those the injured or lost person took. Knowing this, you may want to take greater responsibility for your own safety and self-rescue.

Most experienced people believe that hikers and climbers should not go into the mountains with the conscious or unconscious expectation that someone else will come and rescue them if they get into trouble. They believe that they should pay attention to the risks encountered in hiking, particularly the ones to which they are not exposed in their everyday lives. Consider what your view is in this matter of responsibility concerning rescues. Generate an outlook on rescues and self-rescues, which will form the basis for your decisions in the mountains.

ELECTRONIC AIDS AND THEIR IMPACT

Mountain country becomes a different place when you pull out a "black box" and use it to call for help or to find your way home. With such gear you will not obtain the great satisfaction of self-sufficiency in traveling through the wild, an essential experience for many hikers. The danger in these devices is that they will overcome your cautiousness. They can lead you into extending your hike beyond what is prudent and safe.

These devices alter the experience the wilderness seeker would otherwise enjoy. Passing hikers could overhear your use of a communications device. Other hikers could observe you when you are standing in the open with a navigation device. I urge you to consider the ethic implied when you make the choice to take such gear with you to the mountains. This is not only because of the impact on others, but for your own sake. Even if you do not want a wilderness experience, please do not spoil it for others.

Do not glamorize electronic devices too highly. Keep in mind that electronic gadgets might fail just when you need them. Batteries fail when they are very cold or very hot. The electronic signals on which your device depends may be down because of routine maintenance, or catastrophic failure. You might drop the device and render it useless. You might not be able to send or receive electronic signals in a valley or even a gully, or you might be out of range of the relay tower. You might find that you do not remember the instructions on how to use it. The device might suddenly fail from weathering or corrosion after many years in which you were able to depend on it. If failures of any of your electronic devices do occur, you will appreciate whatever traditional navigation you have done on the way into the wilderness. It is very important to understand that these devices encourage a false sense of security. You really do need to maintain your sense of place and vulnerability, rather than an inflated sense of resources.

GLOBAL POSITIONING SYSTEM (GPS): A GPS receiver relies on satellites to send it information on which to base a calculation of position. It is able to tell you where you are in terms of latitude and longitude (lat/lon). You will find that very few maps show latitude and longitude, and few of those provide a scale for interpolation purposes. This makes it essentially impossible to find on the map the position given by the GPS while you are in the woods or mountains.

Because these devices contain computers that can store positions (waypoints), and can tell you in what direction to go to get to a specific waypoint, they can be useful. If you record the position of your car when you set off into the woods, the GPS can guide you back by providing the direction and distance to your car. Owners of small boats use GPS units to great advantage.

The GPS unit must "see" (have a line of sight to) three or more satellites in order to get sufficient information to compute the lat/lon position. Some units will not work under heavy foliage. Surrounding ridges could block signals from many of the available satellites. The altitude and configuration of the satellites bear on the accuracy of the resulting fix.

The military version of the GPS can provide position information accurate to within about 15 meters or better. When used in conjunction with a sophisticated base station, a GPS unit can give repeatable location results to within a couple of centimeters. The signals used by the handheld units available to civilians give a position fix within 100 meters 95% of the time. The U.S. Government has intentionally degraded the signals available to civilian users under a program called "Selective Availability." The Government might eliminate this degradation in the future.

There was a case in New Hampshire in which a lost hiker called for help on his cellular phone. The rescue authority instructed him over the phone on use of his GPS unit to lead himself back to the trail. Because the resultant direction was uphill, he refused to go. Rescuers had to climb up the mountain and lead him off the high country. Asking for a rescue when you could get off the mountain by yourself is certainly not self-reliance.

CELLULAR PHONES: The day has arrived on which a rock climber, perceiving himself to be trapped on a ledge, has taken a cellular (cell) phone out of his pack and called for help. People have even used cell phones to guide their own rescuers to them. And a hiking friend, who was hard pressed to get his work done before going off with me, pulled out his cellular phone to finish some business while we were on the trail. "It ain't like it used to be!" If you carry a cell phone, people may be able to call you in the middle of the woods. Perhaps the next generation will take "convenience" for granted as a replacement for solitude.

Cell phones have become commonplace. People think of cell phones as being useful anywhere in the mountains, because the user is high in altitude. However, cell phones are dependent upon being reasonably close to, or in view of, a relay transceiver, which is usually on a mountaintop or hilltop. The range is on the order of five miles for low powered systems and ten or twenty miles in hilly country for more powerful systems. The range may be longer under line-of-sight conditions (with nothing in the way between the phone and the relay tower). Satellite based cell phones are limited to line-of-sight conditions.

While cell phones offer the opportunity to call for a rescue immediately after you perceive a need, it may take the rescuers a long time to reach you. If the weather is bad and a helicopter rescue is out, then it might take the rescuers as long as it took you to get to wherever you are. They need some time to organize before they leave, and they will usually have to drive to the trailhead. If you have your phone on all the time the rescue is underway, the batteries may be dead before the rescuers even get close. It is when they are close that you need to talk them toward your location (remember, the weather is bad). Thinking in terms of how long the rescue could take, you should realize that, in bad weather, you might not make it. Do not allow the electronic crutch to lead you into situations from which you cannot retreat.

In February of 1996 an experienced, lone winter hiker lost his way on Mt. Eisenhower (NH). He fell in while trying to descend a brook. His pack contained a low-wattage "flip" type cell phone in a plastic bag with a zipper type closure. We will never know whether or not he tried to use the phone. One man's assessment was that the low power of his phone would probably have been ineffective in the place where they found the hiker.

The victim may have fallen into the brook several times. He soon became too hypothermic to make that call, and he succumbed to the cold. Searchers found him under two feet of water. So having the cell phone with you is not sufficient insurance that you can call for help. You really do need the substantial skill to trail find and navigate when the weather deteriorates.

One could use an age criterion for deciding whether or not to carry a cell phone. If you lead people who are younger than adult age, you might justify carrying an adequate cell phone on the basis of potential liability, or on the basis of what is prudent and customary in your area. The followers do not need to know that you have the cell phone with you. I believe that older people should not expect the same concern, since they choose to take the risk, and are adults. If you are a paid guide the situation changes.

AN ELECTRONIC AID ETHIC: Clearly, the electronic device manufacturers would like you to see the devices as necessary for back country travel. I cannot argue that the devices do not work most of the time, rather that they change the nature of your mountain travel to a lower level of accomplishment and a reduced experience of wilderness. You could extend the same argument to other aids, such as small scale factor maps (7 $1/2$ minute series of USGS topographical maps versus the 15 minute series maps) and thoroughly blazed trails. The important issue to consider is that your mind-set changes when you know you have access to help in your pocket. This can lead you into extending your experience too far through overconfidence. The devices can be something you depend on instead of doing the fundamental navigation and route finding. I urge you to consider carefully what kind of experience it is that you seek, what kind of skill you wish to learn, and who it is you would call. If you do not acquire well-developed skills and knowledge before going to the mountains on your own, you put yourself and others at risk.

IMPACTING THE ENVIRONMENT

The pioneering ethic says that it is heroic to tame the wilderness by cutting the timber, shooting the animals, befouling the streams in the production of useful products, and in making the country "civilized." The preservationist ethic says that we should protect the wilderness and return it to as near a natural state as possible, where there are no man-made structures, where we do not cut the timber, and where the water is not polluted by anyone. The preservationist would limit the number of people who hike through the designated Wilderness Areas and protect the wild inhabitants. This is in order that the traveler's passage would be as close to a wilderness experience as possible. Most of us fall in between these extremes.

These two ethics clash. A compromise resulting from this clash is the multiple use policy of the U.S. Forest Service and the designation of selected, limited Wilderness Areas. In both the designated and non-designated areas of the National Forests where we can camp, how we will avoid water pollution, and when we may use wood fires are limited by rules or guidelines.

Our enjoyment of the wilderness, or our experience of wildness, diminishes when we observe an increase in the number of people and the evidence of their activity. The number of animals we see is likely to rapidly diminish when even a few people begin using their habitat. If we would encourage wild animals to share the wilderness with us, then we should minimize our contact with them.

The number of plant stems broken is likely to be directly related to the number of people bushwhacking. We face the difficult choice of using established, hardened trails and campsites, or diminishing the very wilderness we cherish when we bushwhack through it. We should refrain from off-trail travel particularly during the season when birds and animals seek solitude in which to bear their young (spring and early summer).

Camps for children and leadership schools have found that the maximum group size for good management involves two instructors with every eight students. While we may wish to see smaller groups from an environmental standpoint, a group size of ten has come to be the recommended maximum. However, ten people may be too many when they are camping in the wilderness, or bushwhacking.

Now one can argue that bushwhacking and dispersed camping do not destroy more than nature can rebuild. There is some ability of the environment to rebuild that varies with the types of plants and the terrain. Above tree line, lug soles easily break the soft carpet of lichens and mosses, and it rebuilds slowly. On the other hand, the passage of many feet may not damage open hardwoods with gentle slopes. In the woods, the immediate damage is often related to the steepness of the slope and the lushness of the plants. Longer term damage may result from soil compaction, changes in drainage patterns, root damage, and other impacts.

Nature can repair most environmental damage caused by a party bushwhacking in the wilderness, if we do not make the environment suffer continued assault. From this standpoint, it is important for the wilderness user to avoid using the same campsite or bushwhack route as the previous party. In my view, the least environmental impact will occur, if the party uses established trails and hardened campsites with tent platforms and privies. Since we are not all plant pathologists or experts in environmental causal relationships, it is difficult for us individually to know when our passage through a sensitive area is too much trauma for that specific setting. For this reason I urge you to stay on trails where available, particularly near and above tree line.

Whether we stay on trails, or bushwhack, we can maximize our wilderness experience and minimize our impact by choosing the less traveled country. On several mountains near my home the nicest trails are the longer, less traveled routes on long ridges. Hikers seldom use these trails, and we rarely see signs of anyone else having been through those woods. Often, we see more moose tracks than boot prints. Contrast that with the shorter, overused "herd paths" on the other sides of these same mountains. Enjoy the delightful discovery of wilderness on little used routes.

Vibram® and other cleated boot soles have dramatically increased surefootedness compared to the smooth soles on boots sixty years ago. Of course, they do more to destroy delicate soil and plant structures. Lug soles concentrate the hiker's weight on about sixty percent of the area under the boot. In the rolling action of a normal footstep the lugs act as devices meant to penetrate and tear the soil surface (like a trash compactor at a landfill). We can see lots of wear on trails that have heavy use. The solution for trail protection is hardening using rocks for stepping stones. It may not be either practical, or aesthetically acceptable, to harden whole campsites. It is appropriate for campsite users to wear soft, smooth-soled shoes in camp.

Some portions of our mountains are more sensitive to mans activities than others. In the East all of the plants above and near tree line are living a tenuous existence. Camping here is inappropriate and not permitted. However, the White Mountain National Forest has permitted winter camping above tree line where there is two feet of snow cover over these plants. In the West camping in meadows, particularly alpine meadows, has become inappropriate because of the concentration of people and the sensitive nature of plants there. The shores of alpine ponds are particularly beautiful and desirable places and must also be protected. The few suitable sites high on the peaks with glaciers receive intensive use and need protection from disposal of human waste. There is a problem developing in heavily used campsites below tree line in locations that receive little rainfall during the camping season: the dispersed urine salts smell as much as the privies. I suggest that you use the privies, camp away from and build no fires in sensitive areas, carry out all wrappings and garbage, and use the human waste disposal bags provided for use on glaciers by Park authorities.

Each step off the established trail contributes to the widening of the impacted area. Stepping off the treadway to avoid a wet condition, or ice, widens the trail. It is up to trail maintainers to try to construct or reroute trails so as to minimize the need to get out of the treadway to avoid water or ice. It is up to hikers to use crampons on icy trails in order to avoid the need for walking on the trail border. They should wear footgear in which they can wade when hiking in or after wet weather. It is important to stay on the trail and not walk on the margins making the trail wider.

Hiking during the time that the ground is thawing and soft is particularly damaging to soil structure and plants. Try to avoid hiking during the spring mud season and after heavy rains. Mud season occurs during that period of the year when the surface soil has thawed but lower soil layers remain frozen, trapping water in the upper, saturated soil. Trail soils are in their most sensitive condition from the beginning of the thaw in the spring until early June when all the frost has gone at higher elevations. The Green Mountain Club in Vermont discourages use of its trails during this period.

Some locations remain muddy all year, because the soil remains saturated. This is due to the discharge of groundwater confined by an underlying impervious layer. These soils cannot take more water! Other soils may be mushy after every rain. The hiker can reduce his or her impact on soils by choosing to hike when the soils have thoroughly thawed and the weather is not rainy.

Human noise is something we go to the wilderness to avoid. Others are there for the same reason. Hearing others making loud noises diminishes your wilderness experience. Theirs will be too, if you are inconsiderate. The use of radios and stereo "boom boxes" is inappropriate.

Bright, fluorescent colors stand out in the wilderness, particularly on a cloudy day. These colors are not natural, or foreign. They emphasize man's intrusion, because they bring attention to where people are and where they are camping. Keep this in mind when buying your next piece of equipment or clothing.

Carry out all your trash and whatever you find. Thoroughly bury in soil your excrement *and* toilet paper. Do not cut trees and shrubs, and do not mark anything. Take only pictures. Do not leave footprints in sensitive areas. Leave the natural environment as you found it. We need to learn how to travel so that we leave no sign that we have been there.

Not only should we be nondestructive, we should contribute to maintaining the wilderness in as close to a pristine state as possible. Many people give their due to the wilderness by becoming volunteer maintainers of trails, shelters, and campgrounds. Others work for land protection. Wilderness organizations always need financial support. Each of us needs to adopt wilderness ethics to guide us in the protection of our environment. For guidance see *Backwoods Ethics* and *Wilderness Ethics* by Laura and Guy Waterman.

To obtain a traditional, successful wilderness experience you must use good judgment, a component of which is responsibility. To be responsible you should base your decisions on underlying ethics, and the accompanying rules, thought through in advance. To do that you need to adopt ethics. This is an important undertaking, which I urge you to consider and pursue. Decisions made in the absence of those ethics lack responsibility.

EPILOGUE

Climbing a mountain provides you with an emotional high. The more challenging the mountain, the bigger the high — and the greater the risks. At the extreme, in terms of big mountains, a fraction of the climbers does not survive. You should find it instructional to read what climbers have to say who barely made it down off the mountain. There are many dramatic tales that leave the overall impression of conquest at a cost, such as *Annapurna, The last Blue Mountain*, and *Touching the Void*. Some of these books convey the ethical and moral dilemmas that can occur. Few touch on the emoltional devastation of family and friends following a fatality. I recommend Jon Krakauer's book *Into Thin Air*. It is an account of the 1996 disaster on Mt. Everest in which so many climbers died. The details provide an important example of how goal-driven climbing (peak-bagging) can overcome good judgment. As you read about the tragedy consider what adherence to a turn around time might have meant. You can extend your knowledge and risk management skill, if you take to heart what has happened to others.

Think about the kind of hiker you are. Are you rash, a risk taker, under thirty, and energetic? Forget about being rash. Concentrate on being thoughtful before you act. If you carefully evaluate the risks and how to manage them, you will live to enjoy other adventures. You will reduce the risk to those with you as well as to those who might be called on to rescue you. Further, you will set a positive example for the genera-tion of hikers who will follow you. Using good judgement *is* expected of you, for it may be the differenct between life and death.

Neither gear, skills, knowledge, leadership, nor previous exposure to severe weather alone will make a trip or break it, but combined they make a good foundation. On this foundation you can build great experience and friendship, if you consider what kind of company you are both for yourself and others.

As you go to the mountains consider that they are a treasure to be cherished, respected and protected for our grandchildrens' grandchildren. Washing of feet and dishes in the brook, an accepted practice in the past, is as anachronistic now as bough beds and jodhpurs (once worn by hikers). If the campsite looks worn and dirty, it is because of so many people using it. We are no longer so few in number that we can each have wilderness experience and expect nature to keep pace providing treasure. Each fragile bit of moss above tree line uprooted by lugged soles becomes a sacrifice to human selfishness. Our challenge is to keep the wilderness.

I leave you with three last thoughts:

THERE IS NO ADEQUATE SUBSTITUTE FOR AN EARLY START.

DECISIONS OFTEN MAKE THE DIFFERENCE
BETWEEN LIFE AND DEATH.

A MOUNTAIN TRIP IS SUCCESSFUL
ONLY AFTER A SAFE RETURN.

BIBLIOGRAPHY

The starred references include instructional material pertaining to mountaineering skills.

Angier, B., *How To Stay Alive In The Woods*, MacMillan Publishing Co, Indianapolis, 1962. This book includes description of some of the skills needed for mountain hiking.

Axcell, C., D. Cooke & V. Kinmont, *Simple Foods For The Pack*, Sierra Club Books, San Fransisco, 1986. Delicious menu suggestions. It will get you out of the tuna-fish-and-rice rut.

Bailey, C., *Smart Exercise*, Houghton Mifflin Co., Boston, 1993. A rational exposition on the benefits of exercise. You may also find others of his books helpful.

Barker, R., *The Last Blue Mountain*, The Mountaineers, Seattle, 1959. This is the account of a climb on Mt. Haramosh in the Karakoram region of the Himalaya. The story involves death, courage, and survival by a thin margin.

*Cinnamon, J., *Climbing Rock And Ice*, Ragged Mountain Press, Camden Maine, 1994.

Clark, N., *The Athlete's Kitchen: A Nutrition Guide And Cookbook*, CBI Publishing Co., Boston, 1981.

*Climbing Committee of the Mountaineers, *Mountaineering: Freedom of the Hills*, 5th edition, The Mountaineers, Seattle. General treatment text; source of information about mountaineering techniques.

Damon, R., "White Mountain Avalanche Hazard," *Appalachia*, December, 1970, p. 40. Specific recommendations for specific slopes in NH, plus forecasting pointers.

Day, D.A. & V.J. Schaefer, *Peterson First Guides: Clouds and Weather*, Houghton, Mifflin Co., Boston & New York, 1991. This pocket guide contains lots of pictures and explanation before it gets to forecasting.

*Dunn, J., *Winterwise: A Backpackers Guide*, 2nd Edition, The Adirondack Mountain Club, Inc., Lake George, N.Y., 1996. Highly recommended source of information about winter travel and camping.

Edgington, C.R., & P.M. Ford, *Leadership In Recreation And Leisure Service Organizations*, MacMillan Publishing Co., New York, 1985.

Written for coaches and other leisure sports leaders. Out of print.

Fleming, J., *Staying Found*, 2nd Ed., The Mountaineers, Seattle, 1994.

Fletcher, C., *The Complete Walker*, 3rd edition, Alfred A. Knopf, 1992, Comprehensive work addressed to the hiker rather than the climber.

Getchell, A., *The Essential Outdoor Gear Manual*, Ragged Mountain Press, Camden, ME, 1995.

Gilman, R., "Snowshoes," *Appalachia*, Dec,1969, Includes a discussion of how to make emergency snowshoes.

Goleman, D., *Emotional Intelligence*, Bantam Books, New York, 1995. The author argues that emotional intelligence is much more important than IQ in correlation with personal success.

*Gorman, S., *Winter Camping*, Appalachian Mountain Club Books, Boston, 1991.

Hart, J., *Walking Softly In The Wilderness: The Sierra Club Guide To Backpacking*, Sierra Club Books, 1984 revision. An introduction for beginners to clothing, equipment, trip planning and natural hazards.

Hackett, P.H., *Mountain Sickness: Prevention, Recognition And Treatment*, 6th Edition, The American Alpine Club, New York, 1991. Now distributed by The Mountaineers, Seattle.

Herzog, M., *Annapurna*, Lyons Press, New York, 1997. They successfully made the highest summit to that time, but with near loss of two members of the party.

Hobson, P., *Making And Using Dried Foods*, Storey Communications, Inc., Pownal, Vt., 1994. Includes practical suggestions and menus.

Houston, C., *Going Higher: The Story of Man and Altitude*, Little Brown Publishers, 1987. Unfortunately, this book is currently out of print. It is worth searching for. It deals with the problem of altitude sickness.

Huggins, C.E., "Freezing, Frostbite and Cold Injury," *Appalachia*, December, 1969, p.511.

Irving, L., "Adaption to Cold," *Scientific American*, January, 1966.

Jacobson, D., *The One-Pan Gourmet: Fresh Food On The Trail*, Ragged Mountain Press, Camden, Maine, 1993. Includes a discussion of how to construct an oven out of a 3 pound coffee can. Also has menu and planning ideas.

Kesselheim, A.S., *The Lightweight Gourmet: Drying And Cooking Food For The Outdoor Life*, Ragged Mountain Press, Camden, Maine, 1994.

Kjellstrom, B., *Be Expert With Map And Compass: The Complete Orienteering Handbook*, MacMillan Publishing Co., Indianapolis, 1994 Basic instruction in map and compass use.

Krakauer, J., *Into Thin Air*, Villard, New York, 1997. In 1996 the author was sent by *Outside* magazine to gather material for an article on guided climbs of Mt. Everest. Of the six people in his party who summited, only he (a client) and one guide survived.

*LaChapelle, E. R., *The ABC of Avalanche Safety*, The Mountaineers, Seattle, 1988. This short monograph should be read by everyone who goes to the mountains in the winter and spring.

Lansing, A., *Endurance*, Carroll & Graf, New York, 1959. There is a recent paperback reprint, which does not include the photographs from the original version.

Lentz, M.J., S.C. Macdonald & J.D. Curline, *Mountaineering First Aid*, The Mountaineers, Seattle, 1985.

*Long, J., *Rock Climb*, Chockstone Press, Evergreen, CO., 1993.

McHugh, G., *The Hungry Hiker's Book Of Good Cooking*, Alfred A. Knopf, New York, 1982. Contains instructions on how to dry your own meals for backpacking.

*Powers, P., *NOLS Wilderness Mountaineering*, Stackpole Books, Mechanicsburg, PA, 1993.

*Prater, G., *Snowshoeing*, 3rd edition, The Mountaineers, Seattle, 1988.

Randall, G., *Cold Comfort: Keeping Warm In The Outdoors*, Lyons & Burford, New York, 1987.

Ross, C., & T. Gladfelter, *A Hiker's Companion*, The Mountaineers, Seattle, 1993. Advice on what to take, for long distance hikers.

Rubin, L.D. Sr., & J. Duncan, *The Weather Wizard's Cloud Book*, Algonquin Books, Chapel Hill, N.C., 1989. "How you can forecast the weather accurately and easily by reading the clouds."

Schad, J. & D.S. Moser, Editors, *Wilderness Basics*, 2nd Edition, The Mountaineers, Seattle, 1992 (written by the San Diego Chapter of the Sierra Club).

Seidman, D., *The Essential Wilderness Navigator*, Ragged Mountain Press, Camden, Maine, 1995. This book contains detailed instruction on how to read a map and a compass, as well as, how to navigate.

Simer, P. & J. Sullivan, *National Outdoor Leadership School's Wilderness Guide*, Simon & Schuster, 1985. Helpful guide to weather, clothing, equipment, backcountry travel and first aid.

Simpson, J., *Touching The Void*, Harper and Row, Publishers, New York, 1988. A pair of climbers ascended a 21,000-foot peak in the Andes. One broke his leg and was helped part way down by his partner. They were separated under traumatic circumstances.

Tilton, B., & F. Hubbell, *Medicine For The Backcountry*, ICS Books, Inc., Merrillville, Indiana, 1990. Very succinct coverage of a broad range of topics including bear attacks, high altitude sickness, poisoning, and cold injuries.

Trip Leader Guideline Committee, *A Trip Leader's Handbook: Advice for Successful GMC Outings*, Green Mountain Club, Waterbury, VT, 1997. Good advice for leaders of day hikes. Contains details that are not found here.

Washburn, B., *Frostbite*, Museum Of Science, Boston, 1963.

Waterman, L. & G. Waterman, *Backwoods Ethics: Environmental Issues For Hikers And Campers*, 2nd Edition, The Countryman Press, Woodstock, Vt., 1993.

Waterman, G. & L. Waterman, *Wilderness Ethics: Preserving The Spirit Of Wilderness*, The Countryman Press, Woodstock, Vt., 1993.

Watts, A., *Instant Weather Forecasting*, Dodd, Mead & Co., New York, 1981. Forecasts tied to photographs of current sky conditions.

Weiss, H., *Secrets Of Warmth*, 2nd Edition, Cloudcap, Seattle, 1992. This book is devoted to the art of staying warm, including the physics and physiology. It includes a section on how to dress children so that they will stay warm.

Wilkerson, J.A., C.C. Bangs, & J.S. Hayward, *Hypothermia, Frostbite And Other Cold Injuries*, The Mountaineers, Seattle, 1986.

Worsley, F.A., *Shackelton's Boat Journey*, W. W. Norton & Co., New York, 1977. This is a first person account of Ernest Shackelton's expedition to the Antarctic. The goal of reaching the South Pole was not achieved, but all hands were brought back alive as a result of a lot of luck and some masterful leadership.

_____, "Gear Guide '97," *Backpacker*, March, 1997. This is an annual feature that is quite comprehensive; it should be useful to anyone buying hiking gear.

INDEX